GARDENS
OF THE
CARIBBEAN

Jill Collett and Patrick Bowe

CARIBBEAN

First published 1998 by
MACMILLAN EDUCATION LTD
London and Basingstoke
Companies and representatives throughout the world

ISBN 0–333–68819–8

10 9 8 7 6 5 4 3 2 1
07 06 05 04 03 02 01 00 99 98

This book is printed on paper suitable for recycling and
made from fully managed and sustained forest sources.

Typset by EXPO Holdings, Malaysia

Printed in Hong Kong

A catalogue record for this book is available from the
British Library.

The authors and publishers wish to thank the following for permission to use
copyright material:
Faber and Faber Ltd and Farrar, Straus and Giroux, Inc for Derek Walcott,
'The Star-Apple Kingdom' from *Collected Poems 1948–1984*. Copyright © 1986
by Derek Walcott.
Every effort has been made to trace the copyright holders but if any have been
inadvertently overlooked the publishers will be pleased to make the necessary
arrangement at the first opportunity.

Four prints of Lieutenant John Caddy's (1801–1883) aquatints are reproduced in
this book by kind permission of the Barbados Museum and Historical Society.
Lieutenant Caddy served two tours of duty in the West Indies between 1831
and 1837.

All photographs by Jill Collett, except where otherwise credited.

Cover photographs by Jill Collett

Front cover: Villa Nova, Barbados
Back cover: Francia Plantation, Barbados

❧ CONTENTS ❧

CONTENTS

PREFACE

In this book we aim to celebrate, and to bring to the attention of a wider public, the centuries-old tradition of Caribbean gardening – a tradition that encompasses cottage gardens as well as those of Governor's mansions, contemporary hotel gardens as well as those of historic plantation houses, artists' gardens as well as botanic gardens founded for economic and scientific purposes. Because of their individual historic, geographic and climatic character, no two islands of the Caribbean are alike. Thus each island or group of islands has its own distinctive gardening tradition.

Caribbean gardens also form part of a wider family of tropical gardens located in many other parts of the world. This is illustrated not only by their conception and design but also by their plants. Plants from many of these different areas grow side by side in Caribbean gardens. For example, an African tulip tree may grow alongside an Indian banyan tree; the breadfruit tree, originally a native of Tahiti, alongside a camphor tree from China; a poinciana from Madagascar by a jacaranda from Brazil.

This is the first book to review as a whole the tradition of gardening in the Caribbean. It is written so that little or no formal knowledge of botany and horticulture is required to appreciate it. We hope it will lead to a renewed interest in the conservation of old gardens as well as in the creation of new ones, and also in the conservation of rare garden plants. As in many parts of the world, there is a growing awareness and activity in the gardening world of the Caribbean. We hope this book will help to nourish that growth by giving it a history and a context in which to grow further. New gardens are at present being made (we apologise to garden-makers information about whose creations has come to hand too late to be included in this book). We also hope to stimulate the interest of visitors to, as well as residents of, the Caribbean. The influence that visitors can have on a garden's future is inestimable. Both private owners and government departments respond to increased visitor numbers with increased investment in the expertise, time, money and creative talent required to ensure a garden's development and its future.

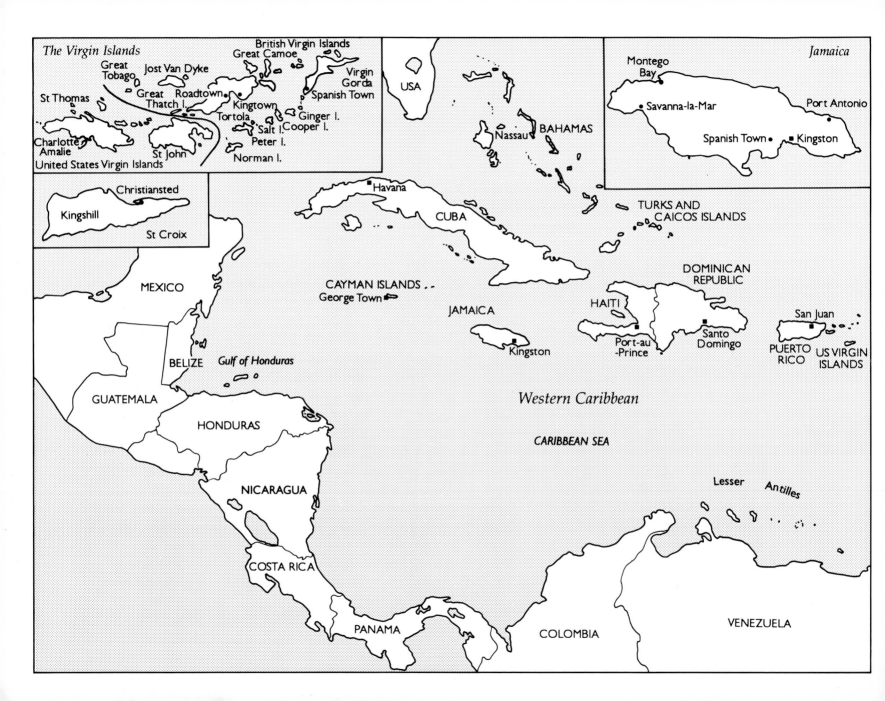

The Virgin Islands

British Virgin Islands
Great Camoe

Great Tobago   Jost Van Dyke

Virgin Gorda
St Thomas   Great Thatch I.   Roadtown   Spanish Town
Charlotte Amalie   Kingtown   Ginger I.
    Tortola   Cooper I.
    Salt I.
    St John   Peter I.
United States Virgin Islands   Norman I.

Christiansted
Kingshill
St Croix

Jamaica

Montego Bay
Savanna-la-Mar   Port Antonio
Spanish Town   Kingston

USA

BAHAMAS
Nassau

Havana
CUBA

TURKS AND CAICOS ISLANDS

DOMINICAN REPUBLIC

CAYMAN ISLANDS
George Town

JAMAICA   HAITI   San Juan
    Kingston   Port-au-Prince   Santo Domingo   PUERTO RICO   US VIRGIN ISLANDS

MEXICO

BELIZE   *Gulf of Honduras*

Western Caribbean

GUATEMALA

HONDURAS   *CARIBBEAN SEA*

NICARAGUA   Lesser   Antilles

COSTA RICA

PANAMA   COLOMBIA   VENEZUELA

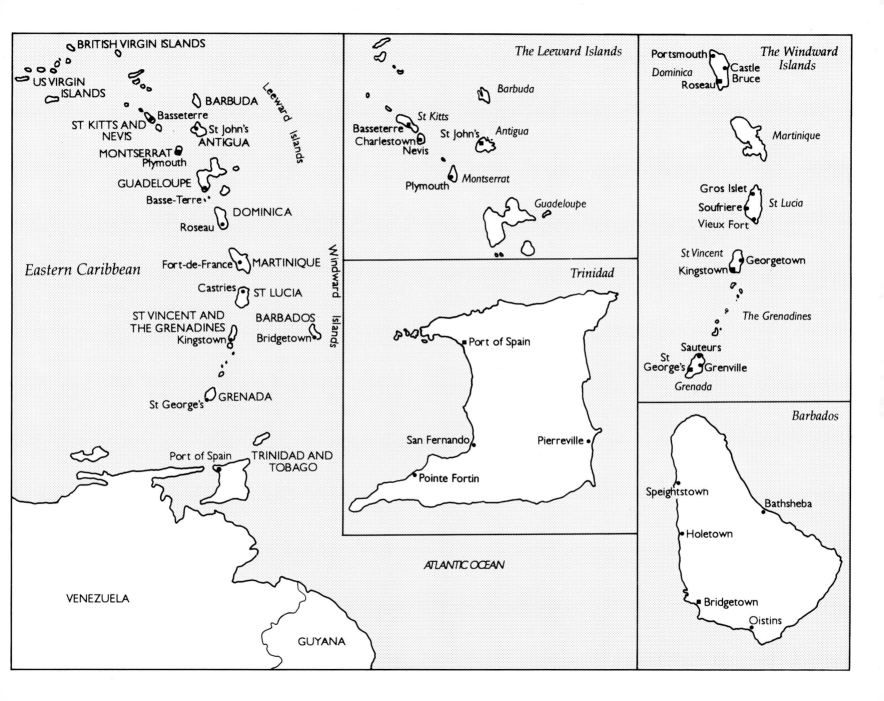

ACKNOWLEDGEMENTS

I would like to thank the staff of the British Museum (Natural History) Library and in particular Dr Dennis Adams who identified plants for me, Mr Tim Cadigan of the Cork Reference Library, the staff of Trinity College Dublin Library and the staff of the Cayman Archives, and Miss Susan Bennett of the Royal Society of Arts Library for all their assistance and encouragement. I would also like to thank Mr David Williams, Director of the Dominica Botanic Garden, Dr Earle Kirby of the St Vincent Botanic Garden, Mr Bhorai Kalloo of the Trinidad Botanic Garden, Miss Helen Hill of Flower Forest, Mr Roy Bennett of Castleton Gardens, Mr Rain Ford of Coyaba and Mr Jonathan Surtees of Strawberry Hill all of whom showed me around personally. I would also like to thank Mr and Mrs Wason, Mr and Mrs Baptiste and Mr and Mrs Aitken with whom I stayed and who gave me great assistance, and Mr Richard Coghlan, Mr Andreas Oberli and Mr Noel Vaucrosson for their suggestions and help without which I would not have achieved so much, and Ms Lavinia Gunn for her help and hospitality in St Vincent. Lastly, my love and gratitude to my daughter Lucy who came with me and looked after me so well.

Jill Collett

I would like to thank Harriet Friedlander who first gave me the opportunity of visiting the gardens of the Caribbean, the late Dr Heino Heine of the Jardin des Plantes, Paris for sharing some of his great knowledge of tropical plants, Valerie Ingram, Librarian at the National Botanic Gardens, Glasnevin, Dublin and Frances-Jane French for their assistance with historical research. I would also like to thank those in the Caribbean who have responsibility for some of the gardens described in the book, in particular, Roberta Williams, Chairperson, Antigua and Barbuda Botanical Gardens Board, Anne Riggall, President of the Botanic Society, Roadtown, Tortola, Joan Devaux and John de Veers, administrators respectively of the Soufriere and Tropicana gardens on St Lucia.

Lastly, I would like to thank G.W. Lennox, Michael Bourne and Pauline Tait at Macmillan Caribbean for supporting the book in every way.

Patrick Bowe

INTRODUCTION

The gardening climate

The Caribbean islands extend in a wide arc about 2,500 miles long from Florida in the north to Venezuela in the south. They lie between latitude 10°N and the Tropic of Cancer and are thus all tropical islands.

Temperatures remain high (77°F/25°C average) throughout the year as does the amount of sunshine ensuring good conditions for plant growth. The seasons are distinguished by variations in rainfall, the summer/rainy season lasting from May/June to October/November and the winter/dry season from December to April. However, climate and growing conditions vary considerably from island to island as a result of their differing topography. For example, a flat island like Antigua has an average rainfall of 40 inches per year whereas mountainous Dominica has an average of 120 inches.

The yellow poinciana is very similar to the red poinciana but is not so widely planted.

On a mountainous island the difference in climate between the windward and leeward sides of the island is very marked. The so-called trade winds blow throughout the year but are particularly strong and steady during the dry winter months. During the rainy season they are moisture-laden and deposit their moisture on the east side of the mountains, leaving the western side quite dry. This results in a marked difference of gardening climate between one side of a mountain and the other. For example, in Jamaica a garden on the windward side will have a rainfall averaging 150 inches per year whereas a garden on the leeward side may get only 60 inches.

The intensity of tropical rainfall is of a different order altogether from the rainfall in non-tropical regions. When cloudbursts are heavy, severe flooding and soil erosion can be serious hazards for the gardener. During the summer and autumn, hurricanes accompanied by very high winds and heavy rains cause great damage to gardens, often destroying decades of careful cultivation. Occasional earthquakes and volcanic eruptions can also cause devastating damage. For example, the botanic garden on the French island of Martinique was destroyed in the cataclysmic eruption of Mont Pelee in 1902. In the drier islands of the southern Antilles such as Barbados prolonged droughts have often resulted in widespread plant mortality. These

climatic hazards render the average life expectancy of gardens and their plants very short. However in a tropical climate they can also regenerate very quickly.

A garden's altitude above sea-level also dictates its character and planting. In the lower coastal areas growth is curtailed during the dry season and trees and shrubs lose their leaves just as they do in temperate-climate gardens during the winter. Salt-laden winds dictate the use of salt-tolerant plants. In the driest areas of all only cacti and other succulents can be grown. In middle-altitude areas a true tropical climate exists. Plant growth continues throughout the year. Trees and shrubs do not shed their leaves at one particular time of the year but rather a few at a time throughout the year. This gives to the gardens in these areas an impression of year-round greenness. Flowering may also take place a little at a time through the year so that the bursts of seasonal blossom associated with temperate-climate gardens are not part of the tropical garden's character.

The differing soil types in the Caribbean also dictate to the gardener what can be grown. For example soils in the volcanic islands are deep, rich and derived from lava. They are acidic in reaction whereas those on the limestone or coral islands are thin, dry and alkaline in reaction. In gardens on the latter soils, for example, citrus fruit trees and hibiscus plants become chlorotic due to the absence of trace elements in the soils.

A view of the wonderful lushness of Caribbean vegetation in Dominica.

ONE

HISTORY OF THE CARIBBEAN AND ITS PLANTS

The movements of the world's prehistoric peoples across the face of the earth may always remain a mystery but it is generally accepted that at some time in the far distant past people crossed the Bering Straits, from Mongolia and Asia, which was perhaps a land bridge at that time, and made their way down the length of North America, down the Isthmus of Panama to South America. Some scattered on the way, peeling off to become the American Indians, some went on to the Caribbean islands. There is an elaborate, evocative map in the Museum of Anthropology in Mexico City to convince the viewer of this.

The first known occupants of the Caribbean islands were the Arawaks. They were a peaceful people. Physically they were smaller than the Caribs who were to conquer them later. They were also weaker, possibly because they were not used to hard physical labour. They lived what sounds like an idyllic existence in the islands and ate what today would be regarded as a very correct diet. The protein in their diet consisted of fish, shellfish, turtle, manatee, agouti, iguana and duck. (Manatee is a herbivorous sea creature, a sea-cow; an agouti is a hare-like creature and an iguana a lizard-like miniature dragon.) They grew a good range of fruit such as pineapples, mammees, starapples, naseberries, guavas and cashews. Their vegetables were maize, cassava, sweet potato, yautia and groundnut. They knew how to stew, bake and roast their food and they smoked fish, using salt produced from salt pans or pools, and pepper (the small red hot peppers) for seasoning. From cassava juice, salt and pepper they made cassareep which is still used as a Caribbean sauce and preservative. They also made pepperpot, another Caribbean dish still in use. (Pepperpot is a meat and vegetable stew made over several days. Each day more ingredients are added and the pot is always kept on the back of the stove.) They grew cotton from which they made their hammocks, one of their few furnishings, and tobacco for chewing, pipes and cigars. They went naked in the warm climate (except for married women who wore a loin cloth) though they wore leg bands dyed to different colours. The babies' heads were bound in infancy to achieve the narrow, slightly pointed shape considered beautiful.

Hope Gardens in Jamaica where bougainvillea flourishes.

Both men and women wore elaborate make-up. The houses they built were round with walls of woven creepers and canes; the roofs were conical and thatched with straw. Conch shells were blown to summon people or attract attention.

Columbus described the Arawaks' smooth brown skin as 'olive'. Their hair was coarse, straight, thick and black and was worn long. The make-up, which was black, white and coloured, was used as body paint. They did have some gold jewellery. Presumably the gold must have come from South America, or possibly Hispaniola or Cuba. They believed in an after-life, a heaven, and they prayed to their ancestors to relieve their earthly troubles.

Into this relatively sophisticated society came the Caribs from South America, gradually moving northwards up the island chain. In many ways they were very similar to the Arawaks but Carib society was slightly less sophisticated, rougher and more war-like. In appearance they were larger and fitter than the Arawaks. They were not such good farmers but they built better canoes in which they travelled long distances, and they were better fishermen. They had many similar customs but did not use salt, although they used plenty of pepper and made pepper sauces. They also made and drank a great deal of cassava beer. Later the Caribs were to claim they had killed the previous inhabitants of the islands. Physically they have been described as being 'of good stature and well proportioned', with long, black, thick hair and the same flattened heads of the Arawaks. Their brown skin appeared more red than that of the Arawaks from the roucou dye which was freshly applied every day. The fruit of the genip gave a black dye.

The Carib temperament was different from that of the Arawaks. They were rather melancholic, unsmiling and silent, although they were very agile and strong, and excellent swimmers. Descriptions are given of their canoes overturning which discommoded them not at all as the men swam about and collected the luggage while the women, carrying their babies, patiently waited for the canoe to be righted. Their melancholic temperament led, however, to anomalies. Although generous with each other in sharing possessions, when in their cups they murdered each other without thought. A grudge might be borne silently until, perhaps after a shared meal, the object of the grudge would suddenly be murdered. This led inevitably to feuds and there seems to have been no taboo about such behaviour, and no punishment. They were undoubtedly cannibals, although this was reserved for their male enemies and victims in war. The men were killed, cooked and eaten but the women, although captured, were treated gently, taken as wives and any children were reared with the children of the group of Caribs. This custom led to the strange fact that the women spoke a different language to the men, particularly amongst themselves. There is a description of an old woman inciting the warriors to anger by the recitation of past wrongs and the deaths of relations and finally throwing cured limbs of male captives into the middle of the assembly, which were then eaten.

The Caribs' diet seems to have been just as good as the Arawaks'. They did not have cattle, sheep, goats, pigs or poultry (much to the astonishment and interest of the Spaniards) and therefore ate no cheese, milk, eggs, butter, oil or fat. They did eat turtle eggs, crabs, some birds and

fish. They made stews and boiled the crabs but always bar-becued fish and birds whole, with the feathers and scales on and the guts still in. The result was juicy and succulent. They also smoked food. There is a good description of a 'coffer fish' or box-fish being cooked whole. They, like the Arawaks, had salt pans but did not use the salt for season-ing. Their pepper sauce, made with boiled manioc and lemon juice with a lot of crushed pepper, was very hot. They grew sweet potatoes, manioc and cassava, which was made into cassava bread; at feasts for assemblies there were also yams, bananas and figs. There was a more innocuous drink than cassava beer made from crushed pineapple and another made of honey and water. Like the Arawaks, the Caribs grew tobacco.

Into this world arrived the Spaniards. (They have given us the details of the American Indian's lives. Columbus also left careful accounts and Dr Chanca, surgeon to the voyage sent descriptions home to Spain.) The Portuguese were the first European explorers of the Far East, India, China, the islands of the Pacific and the coast of Africa. The Spaniards were envious of the wealth it brought them. With the improvement in both navigational instruments and ship design they were able to contemplate mounting explo-rations for themselves. They looked to the west where it was claimed there was another continent. There was a certain amount of opposition from the church as the explor-ers' discoveries might conflict with church teaching about the world and its origins. The explorers were encouraged to go only in order to convert the heathens they encountered. The winds and currents were favourable for reaching the

Bananas are one of the staple crops of the Caribbean.

West Indies and the Americas from Europe even though the return passage was much more difficult. The trade winds influenced the importance of different islands. Barbados, set slightly further out into the Atlantic, had to be visited before the other islands as it could not be returned to on the homeward passage because of the winds which took the ships through more northerly passages. This was also a protection for Barbados.

Columbus is believed to be the first European to make the voyage to the Caribbean. His first sight of land was San Salvador in the Bahamas chain. Its Indian name was Guanahani. He mentions finding plenty of 'aloe' growing there. He left a description of Hispaniola and Cuba, how well wooded they were, with fine rivers and good harbours.

Red aloe has always been prized for its medicinal uses and is still popular today. Columbus' 'aloe' was almost certainly not this plant. All *Aloe* spp are Old World or originated there.

He saw six or eight different kinds of palms growing as well as spices, and thought the land must be very fertile. There were plenty of birds. He also described mines of gold with traces of gold in the rivers. He mentions honey – before the widespread use of sugar-cane, this was a valuable sweetener and preservative. He had ample time to observe all this as he built his first settlement on Hispaniola after the loss of his flag ship.

Columbus also described the simple palm-thatched houses of the Caribs as being surrounded by gardens *as pleasant as they are in Castile in May* and by tilled land in which beans and maize were sown. The settlers who accompanied Columbus on his subsequent transatlantic voyages noted the Caribs' techniques in cultivating food plants and also realised the potential for improving the wild fruits, vegetables and herbs which the Caribs gathered to bring them into garden cultivation. The settlers brought with them from Europe seeds of their own food plants, such as melons, cucumbers, oranges and sugar-cane. Columbus records how astonished they were by how quickly they were ready for harvesting in the tropical climate and fertile soils.

Columbus made his second voyage in 1494. This was recorded by Dr Chanca, doctor to the Spanish Royal family, who went on the voyage as surgeon to the expedition. The first landfall was Dominica and they then sailed north to Nevis and Guadeloupe. Dr Chanca described mountains with beautiful woods right down to the water's edge and mentions the allspice trees. He refers to the very high mountains of Guadeloupe and the many rivers and waterfalls. One in particular had a very large torrent of water from

The strong smell of allspice contributes to men's toiletries.

a narrow opening. The Spaniards went ashore and, as the inhabitants had fled temporarily, they entered their houses. They found cotton ready for spinning and cloth of good quality, plus a new kind of parrot (of which they took two). Dr Chanca claimed there was plenty of evidence of cannibalism. The expedition then sailed north past Montserrat, which was uninhabited, Antigua, Nevis, the Virgin Islands and Puerto Rico. Some of these islands were still inhabited at that date by Arawaks who were so terrified of the Caribs that they were inclined to flee at the sight of any visitors.

Columbus, in spite of his great discoveries, made various serious mistakes in his dealings with both the Arawaks and Caribs. Labour was necessary for the development of the islands and the Europeans could not provide it in sufficient quantity because there were too few of them and because of their inability to work in such heat. Forced labour was regarded as the answer. The Papal Bull of 1493 ignored the rights of the Indians because they were not subjects of a Christian Prince. On the other hand Isabella, Queen of Spain, seems to have been merciful for the age, and repudiated slavery which was what the forced labour had become. Various laws were passed to try to protect the Indians and it was expected they would be converted to Christianity. What was not realised was that the Arawaks were not physically capable of hard manual labour, not being used to it as they had never found it necessary. The Caribs would not be slaves – they would rather die. They committed suicide if necessary and killed their children too. The Spaniards practised every cruelty on the Arawaks, including burning them alive. They also killed them from starvation by forcing them to neglect their crops. It was genocide of the Arawaks by the Spaniards. It was not until 1502 that any proper administration was set up by the Spaniards. Before that the settlers would not accept any authority. The extermination of the Arawaks continued and, when there was a labour shortage, the Lucayos from the Bahamas were drafted in – and treated in a similar fashion.

Hispaniola became the central Spanish island settlement for a while, with relatively sophisticated standards, although by 1580 there were many small Spanish settlements on various islands, particularly Dominica and bigger ones on Puerto Rico. To some extent the tables were turned when Spaniards were captured by the Caribs and kept as prisoners and slaves – or eaten. There had been a certain amount of livestock brought from Spain by the first settlers and they were able to breed from these. From this came cattle ranching and beef, pork and mutton were produced. Some of this produce was sold to passing ships but there was surplus. European crops such as vines, olives and wheat would not grow and the settlers had to rely on rice, yams and cassava, although figs, oranges, lemons and bananas grew well.

Jamaica was settled in 1509. It was used for supplying passing ships with meat, hides and tallow from the cattle on the island, though the island itself was not regarded as very important. By the late sixteenth century the trade in slaves from Sierra Leone had been established. This, of course, solved the labour crisis. By 1565 a French colony had been established on the Florida coast, which must have caused the Spanish some unease.

This is shell ginger (*Zerumbet speciosum*). It has no culinary uses unlike ginger (*Zingiber officinale*).

P M Anglerius' 1577 account of his travels in the West Indies adds the date palm and the pomegranate to the list of plants brought into cultivation from Spain. The potential of the area for the cultivation of food plants, in particular sugar and spices, was becoming well-known throughout Europe. For example, when Sir Walter Raleigh arrived off the coast of Trinidad in 1532, he saw growing *sufficient maize, cassivi* (sic) *and of those other rootes and fruites which are common everywhere in the West Indies* and also observed the excellent soil which *will beare sugar, ginger or any other commoditie that the Indies yield*. The term 'Indies' was at that time used to mean not only India itself but also much of south-east Asia.

Sugar – the crop that was to affect Caribbean history so traumatically – was originally grown in Cyprus and Spain in Europe, having come from the Far East. It was then tried in the Canaries and finally in 1493 it was taken to the Caribbean where it grew very successfully. However, various problems faced the settlers over its cultivation. People from the Canary Islands had to be brought over to teach the settlers how to cultivate it and use the necessary technology. High investment was needed for the sugar mills and the plantations and money was lent by the government for this. The first mill was built in 1516 and the need for a large labour force was solved by the importation of the slaves.

By 1530 sugar was a well-established industry but it was a monoculture and the population relied on food imported from Spain. Reliance on imported food from the mother country affected many of the new settlements and colonies. Part of the problem of colonialism was that the mother country expected the colonists only to sell their produce to her. There were also no favourable tariffs (duties) applied to produce from other countries so the colonists were not protected in their trade and the balance was weighted in favour of the mother country. In some cases the newly cultivated land of the islands became worked out and impoverished – often through ignorance, laziness and lack of inclination for farming. It seemed much easier to buy food from abroad than struggle to cultivate it locally. The problems of the Spanish islands and settlements of the sixteenth century were to be repeated in the British settlements of the seventeenth and eighteenth centuries. In the Spanish settlements, the sugar industry was in decline by 1600 because the Spanish government would not ban competition from Brazil. One other aspect of the history of Spain in the Caribbean must be touched on – that of the large quantities of gold transported to Spain in the great galleons. Many defensive ports and castles were built at strategic points and elaborate measures were taken to protect the great treasure ships – most did get home safely. In spite of all the stories and romances the pirates did not really capture that many ships.

The religious Reformation in seventeenth century Europe had its affect on the history of the Caribbean. It divided the European states into Roman Catholic and Protestant, with the Protestant states determined to break the Spanish monopoly of the Caribbean. Elizabeth I of Protestant England encouraged her privateers, in the persons of Hawkins and Drake, to raid and try to break the power of Catholic Spain. This was not for entirely religious reasons but because Spain refused to allow cheaper goods from England, France and Holland to be sold to the Spanish settlers. There existed at this time a monopoly on trade in the East and Far East by the Portuguese and in the West by the Spanish. The Protestant Dutch had entered the scene and had declared war on Spain, the Dutch being secretly supported by Elizabeth. The Dutch were also trading in the Far East by this time, having taken over the spice trade from the Portuguese. This led to the formation of the East India Company and the West India Company.

The Dutch started in the West by trading salt from salt mines in Venezuela and they were involved in the slave trade from West Africa. They took over Brazil and there learned to produce sugar, a skill they passed on to the English and French who had arrived in the Caribbean. It was the era of great ship building by the Dutch – by 1623 800 Dutch ships were trading. It was the Dutch who were responsible for breaking the Spanish monopoly and this encouraged other nations with small colonies to prosper.

All English colonies were proprietor-owned to start with. The English king was not interested in the problems of new possessions as long as he got the taxes. However as the seventeenth century progressed, increasing administration had to be set up to deal with these colonies because of trade. In 1672 the Council for Trade and Plantations was established. This had been preceded in 1663 by an Act declaring that all English possessions would become Crown Colonies. This established a Governor for each, a House of Assembly took the place of the House of Commons and a Governor's Council that of the House of Lords. In fact it became a more intimate body on whom the Governor relied but on occasions also had bitter disagreements with. The Governors' salaries were very small and they were expected to make money from privileges such as the sale of whale oil, or duties paid on certain commodities. The Assemblies were regarded as very important by the colonists but there were always arguments over money and duties paid on exports which irritated the planters. Local militias provided defence for each island, not only against invasion from outside, but against slave revolts internally and any form of civil strife. The colonists were expected to serve in the militias and white indentured servants were co-opted. In some instances trusted black slaves were armed as well.

In the seventeenth and eighteenth centuries the colonies were regarded as farms for the mother country, able to supply commodities that were not available in Britain such as sugar, tobacco, tropical crops and spices. In return Britain supplied manufactured goods. Many shopping lists exist of goods sent for from Britain which include everything from shoes and materials to saddlery for horses and coal for fires. The only problem with this arrangement was that the colonies could only buy and sell with Britain.

The increasing prosperity of the European settlers led to a more sumptuous way of life. The 1655 narrative of General Venables mentions an avenue of orange trees on Hispaniola which was seven miles long. He also records how, when his ship was anchored in the harbour of Santo Domingo, the capital of Hispaniola, *every night was borne a most delicious scent from the shore by the land wind as could possibly be smelt of the fruits, blossoms and herbs of the towne, there being many gardens joyning to the houses.*

Exotic plants continued to be imported for cultivation. Several, unnamed, Indian palms as well as the Arabian tamarind tree are recorded in Barbados by 1647. Since Columbus' time the preferred sea-route from Europe to the Caribbean had been via the West African coast and the Canary Islands. On the latter, tropical Asian plants like sugar-cane had been cultivated for some time and it was from the Canary Islands via Brazil that sugar-cane ultimately reached the Caribbean.

The seventeenth century also brings the first reference to a professional gardener working in the area – a Mr Willisal who in 1674 was gardener to John Vaughan, third Earl of Carberry in Jamaica. The century also brought the first systematic botanical exploration when Sir Hans Sloane, the Irish physician and plant collector, travelled to the West Indies with the Governor of Jamaica in 1687. He returned to London with 800 plant specimens which he described in a catalogue published in 1696.

In his book *Nouveau Voyage aux isles de l'Amerique* (A New Journey to the American Isles) published in 1722, the French Dominican, Père Labat, described the formal avenues of tamarind trees which led to the plantation houses of Barbados and the large shaddock trees with which the houses were surrounded to protect them from the intense heat of the sun. Ten years later, an anonymous traveller in the Antilles wrote of the formal avenues of orange trees in and around the capital of Martinique, St Pierre. In his book *The Natural History of Barbados* (1750), Griffith Hughes describes the cabbage palm walks which surrounded the island's plantation houses. The spectacular cabbage palm avenue at Codrington College is probably the best surviving example.

Gardening activity on a plantation was, however, not confined to the ornamental grounds. A provision ground providing food formed part of most plantations and the slaves laboured on them as they did on the rest of the plantation. According to Père Labat, writing in 1722, fruits such as limes, sour oranges, guavas, soursops, papayas and mangoes, and vegetables such as yams, plantains, peppers, cassava and guinea corn, were growing in them. However, H N Coleridge in his book *Six Months in the West Indies* (1826) relates how the slaves on Barbados had no provision grounds but *gardens of their own which they might cultivate as they please: either yams, Indian corn, plantains or even canes are to be seen around every hut.*

Janet Schaw also described the view beyond the house in which she stayed on Antigua: *The fields all the way down to the town are divided into cane pieces by hedges of different kinds. The favourite seems the log-wood, tho' extremely beautiful, is not near so fit for the purpose as what is called the prickly pear which grows into a fence so prickly and close as hawthorn.*

During the seventeenth and eighteenth centuries slavery became an even more marked way of life in the islands of the Caribbean. The economy of the islands rested entirely on slave labour. The slaves became the necessary evil for the working of the sugar plantation. Arawaks and Caribs had been tried by the Spaniards. White indentured servants were not satisfactory because they would not work with black people, and in any case left when their indentures were finished. There was a plentiful supply of slaves

Tamarind trees live to a great age. Their fruit is used in sauces and cool drinks.

11

This handsome avenue of cabbage palms at Codrington College in Barbados is duplicated many times throughout the Caribbean.

from Africa and, in spite of the fact so many died on the voyage, within the first year or soon after, this was regarded as the solution to the labour problem. It must be remembered that slavery was an accepted concept for the age. Economics overrode every other consideration.

Dutch supremacy in trade in the Caribbean was being challenged by England by the middle years of the seventeenth century. France also wanted territory and harassed the English colonies and took over islands. The Caribs joined in the general mêlée and raided and pillaged. There is a suspicion that the French used them as allies and managed to befriend them in a way that escaped the English. By the early eighteenth century France and Britain were equals in the Caribbean, the Dutch having been ousted, but islands changed hands back and forth with great frequency.

The British colonies were more productive, but the French had more land. The British had two naval bases in Antigua and Jamaica and France none till 1784. The various wars of the eighteenth century did have a bad effect on the islands, and some never recovered because planters were killed and slaves carried off, leaving no labour to restart plantations. By 1759 the British were in command of the Caribbean but by the Treaty of Paris in 1763 many islands were restored to previous owners. There had been a sugar boom in the British islands between 1748 and 1756 but after 1763 the French islands started to increase production. By the Sugar Act of 1764 duties on sugar were lowered in the British islands but they had to pay a tax which was carefully collected.

The American War of Independence 1776–1783 had a bad effect on the islands as Britain found herself fighting not only her colony, America, but France, Spain and Holland as well. Although the British islands were sympathetic to America, having many of the same grievances, they did not rebel because they needed the protection of the British Navy. The most serious effect of the war was the cutting of trade links with America. The West Indies were deprived of timber, saltfish, meat, grain and rice. The slaves suffered most and there was general famine. After the war, Canada tried to take the place of America but duties were higher than previously. The war of independence in Haiti (1791 onwards) also had far-reaching effects, not only for herself but also for other islands. In 1791 Haiti was the leading exporter of sugar at 73,000 tons which decreased by 1804 to 20,500 tons and by 1825 to one ton. The events in Haiti were watched by other slave societies with both admiration and nervousness. There was a great exodus of planters from Haiti, some going to the other islands, some to America. The Napoleonic Wars started in 1793 and ran till 1802, starting again in 1803 after a brief respite. Napoleon ordered attacks on the West Indies and sugar convoys, without much success. Once again islands changed hands and were invaded and then changed hands again.

Although the eighteenth century was a time of great upheaval and many skirmishes and invasions, it was also an era of great prosperity for some. Handsome houses were built by the planters, many of cut stone blocks with high handsome rooms, local wood doors, large windows and deep shady verandas. The architectural style of the houses closely followed contemporary styles in Europe, as did the gardens which were formally laid out with parterres, walks and avenues. There were plenty of slave servants and life

Lieutenant Caddy's picture of Castries, St Lucia. The island was famed for its curative mineral baths in the eighteenth century.

was leisurely. The rooms of the houses contained furniture made of local woods as well and as elegantly as any procurable from Britain. Hospitality was lavish with silver on the dining tables and gleaming glass. Much was sent from Britain including ready-made clothes. Cut material by the yard was also sent to be made up by the local seamstresses.

In the towns gardening was flourishing, in parks and squares, in churchyards and cemeteries as well as in private gardens. Janet Schaw writes of the townhouses of Basseterre on St Kitts as having *pretty parterres before them*. She goes on to describe how one of them was shaded with *cocoa or palmetto trees* and how another had an orange grove behind it. Charles Kingsley, the nineteenth century author whose best known novel is *The Water Babies*, writes of a 1796 description of Castries, the capital of St Lucia with *its neat cottages, smiling flower gardens, smooth grass-plots and gravel walks.*

Flower gardens were also formal. In *The Journal of a Lady of Quality* (1774–6), Janet Schaw gives a delightful description of an Antiguan plantation garden:

My bed-chamber, to render it more airy, has a door which opens into a parterre of flowers that glow with colours, which only the western sun is able to raise into such richness, while every breeze is fragrant with perfumes that mock the imitations to be produced by art. This parterre is surrounded by a hedge of pomegranate which is now loaded both with fruit and blossom.

By 1750, gardens with formal avenues, walks and parterres were going out of fashion in Europe and being replaced by informal layouts with curving, serpentine walks and greater horticultural variety. Janet Schaw's diary describes a Mr Freeman's garden in Antigua which boasted this new informal style. Serpentine rather than straight walks led to the house, avenues were planted not with just one tree variety but many, such as oranges, citrons, limes, coconuts, myrtles and palmetto. The garden itself was characterised not by a formal layout but by its horticultural richness and included a carnation tree, cape jasmine, flowering cedar, the four-o'clock shrub and a variety of passion flowers. A good example of the informal style of landscaping can be experienced in Antigua at Clarence House, built in 1786 to house the Duke of Clarence (later William IV) when he was serving in the Royal Navy at nearby English Harbour.

Increased prosperity also resulted in the development of town planning and the capitals of many of the islands were graced by formal squares and tree-lined avenues. Among the most elegant squares is that of Spanish Town on Jamaica which is surrounded by towering royal palms – as is the twelve-acre Savane in Fort-de-France, the capital of Martinique. Place de la Victoire in Point-a-Pitre, the capital of Guadeloupe, is lined with palms, poincianas and sandbox trees. In Columbus Square in Castries, St Lucia there is a monumental saman tree. The tiny park at the end of the main street in Charlotte Amalie, St John boasts a group of lignum vitae trees. The layout of many Caribbean squares is focused on a commemorative statue, such as that of the Empress Josephine in Fort-de-France or Felix Aboue in Point-a-Pitre. Less solemn are the squares focused on elaborate Victorian cast-iron fountains, often gaily painted, such as that in Independence Square in Basseterre, St Kitts or the cast iron clock at Plymouth, Montserrat. Among the most attractive tree-lined streets and alleys are those lined with cabbage palms such as those leading into Independence Square at Basseterre, St Kitts and the one-kilometre long Allee Dumanoir in Guadeloupe, lined with royal palms. On Guadeloupe is the Allee des Flamboyants which is lined with flame trees spectacular when in flower from May to September.

Also contributing to the graceful environment of many towns are the tree-plantings around several churches and their graveyards. Outstanding are the huge tamarind trees around St John's Cathedral in Antigua and the flame trees planted around St Peter's Church, also in Antigua. St George's Cathedral in St Kitts is surrounded by its own garden, while St Thomas' Church, also in St Kitts, is approached along an avenue of royal palms. St James'

The graveyard at the Trinidad Botanical Gardens.

Churchyard in Barbados is described by Griffith Hughes in 1750 as having a cedar of Lebanon growing in it, presumably with a view to replicating the planting of some English country churchyard.

Two factors were to change life in the islands. One was the feeling in Britain that the sugar interests were too powerful and too privileged. Quite a few seats in the House of Commons were controlled by the planters and they fought for favourable duties. The concept of free trade was in the air and a sugar industry had been started in Louisiana and in India. Cuba had become the successor to Haiti. What was to have a more far-reaching effect was that Prussia had started growing sugar beet.

The other factor was that the wars had demonstrated how vulnerable the islands were to blockade and loss of trade in food. It was realised how little food for the local populations was grown on the islands. In 1758 the London-based Society for the Encouragement of Arts, Manufactures and Commerce, which had been founded in 1754 and was later to be called The Royal Society for Arts, offered rewards for the improvement of agriculture and horticulture in the 'American colonies'. A prize was offered for the first person to bring mango seeds to England for onward shipment to the West Indies. In 1760 the list of plants included olives, opium, cinnamon, nutmeg, mace, sarsaparilla, aloe, safflower, indigo, cotton, annatto, vanilla, cloves, pepper, camphor, quinine, various tinctorial plants and ornamental woods. Many of the planters tried individually to import the plants, not just for the prizes offered but for the potential marketing of profitable crops. It so happened that the then Governor of St Vincent, General Melville, was also a member of the Society for Arts and in 1765 he, at his own expense, bought a piece of land and cleared it in order to set up a botanic garden, which was the first in the Caribbean. Jamaica soon decided it wanted such a garden and was lucky enough to have a planter who started his own collection of imports. The Society offered to start a garden in the Bahamas but the offer seems to have fallen on stony ground and there never has been a botanic garden there.

The Society's influence led to the famous journey by Captain Bligh in the *Bounty* in search of breadfruit from the South Seas. It was thought that this would make a good additional food for the slaves of the Caribbean. New types of sugar-cane were introduced about this time and were so successful that in 1806 there was a glut. Napoleon closed European ports to British ships but the War of 1812 stopped trade by American ships and England once again had a boom. Cotton became a successful crop in the West Indies but the invention of the cotton gin in America affected that trade because less slave labour was needed.

The effect of the Abolition of Slavery in the nineteenth century had as great an impact and created as much of a social revolution as the introduction of sugar did in the seventeenth century. The movement to abolish slavery started in the eighteenth century. There always had been people who found it unacceptable and morally wrong. By the 1780s and 90s such feelings were gathering momentum with the help of missionaries who were mostly non-conformists. The first steps had been to try to improve conditions for the slaves but there was great opposition from the planters. Orders from Britain were ignored by Jamaica, Barbados, St Vincent and Dominica. Reform for the conditions of all lower classes in all societies was in the air, largely brought about by the Industrial Revolution which transformed an agricultural society into an urban one.

The Emancipation Act of 1833 freed the slaves and suggested an apprenticeship scheme instead. The idea did not work – some islands tried it but others did not. Monetary compensation was paid to the planters for their slaves which varied from island to island in proportion to productivity. But the apprenticeship scheme had to be abolished altogether. After emancipation there was a labour problem, of course, and this too varied from island to island. In some islands the slaves refused to go back to the plantations even for money, in others they were prepared to work again. In the larger islands where there was plenty of land, so that the slaves could own some themselves, it was more of a problem than in the smaller islands where there was no alternative way of making a living than working on the plantations. Subsistence farming was possible on some islands growing cassava, maize, sweet potato, pineapple, paw paw and bananas, which became an important subsistence crop. It was at this point that the importance emerged of what had been encouraged at the end of the eighteenth century – the importation of additional new crops. Ackee, breadfruit and mango are some of the most obvious. However money was necessary to buy salt meat and salt fish and this forced the ex-slaves into some labour for others. The slaves desperately wanted to own land. This the planters at first resisted, fearing it would make labour even more difficult to obtain, but in spite of this the ex-slaves did manage to acquire it gradually. Once again it

Originally brought from Africa, the ackee is now so popular that it is the official fruit of Jamaica.

17

varied in different islands. Where they stayed on their original estates, rent for cottages was usually cheaper if they worked there – and wages varied. In some cases fringe benefits were retained as in the days of slavery. It eventually turned out that some islands were able to grow more sugar than before emancipation. Britain still wanted to maintain the sugar trade so it had to help over labour problems and suggest new immigrants for the purpose. European labour, Scots and Irish, proved to be useless as the climate was too hot, the labour too hard and the labourers had no resistance against tropical diseases. People from Madeira and Malta suffered the same problems. Some free African labour was tried but the system was open to abuse. Chinese labour also proved disastrous because the recruiting agents deceived them at the time of recruitment. Finally it was the Indians from India who solved the problem and large numbers were brought to the islands from 1838 onwards. The system was also open to abuse but in balance it can be regarded as successful and their descendants today probably feel the same.

During the Napoleonic Wars the British West Indies had a near monopoly in sugar production and prices were high but after the war new producers emerged. There was competition from India, Cuba, Louisiana, Brazil and Mauritius. The planters had not adjusted themselves and failed to mechanise and modernise. The industry was labour intensive, there were no ploughs, pitchforks or wheelbarrows even by 1846. Trinidad and British Guyana were the exceptions. Additionally, although sugar beet was expensive to produce, the countries of Europe were prepared to subsidise the industry in order to be free of Caribbean sugar and to provide employment.

Yet one positive trend is identifiable – that of the development of new cottage gardens by the freed slaves. They often attracted the attention of visitors. The novelist, Anthony Trollope described them with great enthusiasm in his book *The West Indies and The Spanish Main* (1859):

They are not filled, as a peasant's garden in England or in Ireland is filled, with potatos and cabbages, or other vegetables similarly uninteresting in their growth; but contain cocoa-trees, breadfruit trees, oranges, mangos, limes, plantains, jack-fruit, soursop, avocado, pears and a score of others, all of which are luxuriant trees, some of them of considerable size, and all of them of great beauty.

The writer, Charles Kingsley, was also entranced and wrote in his book *At Last, A Christmas in the West Indies* (1871) of the variety of fruit, vegetables and seeds which were being grown. Of fruits, he saw oranges, breadfruits, mangoes, mamees, starapples, avocados, sapodillas, roseapples, sweet-sops and guavas. Of vegetables, he saw bananas, plantains, cassavas, pigeon-peas, yams, arrowroots and sweet potatoes as well as castor oil and maize. Of seeds he saw, he mentions French physic nut, Indian shot, earth nut, okra and pumpkin. Of the owner of a cottage garden he writes:

If he be a prudent man, he will have a plant of the pretty Overlook pea (Canavalia) trailing aloft somewhere to prevent his garden from being 'overlooked' i.e. bewitched by an evil eye, in case the Obeah-bottle which hangs from the mango tree, charged with toad-spider, dirty water and so forth has no terrors for his secret enemy.

The last section of Kingsley's description of the garden of the typical Trinidadian cottager's garden is devoted to the flowers which he grew in it:

... his hedge will be composed of Hibiscus bushes, whose magnificent crimson flowers contrast with the bright yellow bunches of the common Cassia, and the scarlet flowers of the Jumby bead bush (Erythrina corallodendron) *and the blue and white and pink convolvulus. The sulphur and purple Neerembergia of our hothouses, which is here one mass of flower at Christmas and the creeping crab's eye vine* (Abrus precatorius) *will scramble over a fence; while as a finish to his little paradise, he will have planted at each of its four corners an upright Dragon's blood bush* (Dracaena terminalis) *... here used from their unlikeness to any other plant in the island, to mark boundaries.*

Dracaena (*Cordyline fruticosa*) is here being used as a boundary marker on St Vincent.

As a result of the burden of debt in the islands, two Royal Commissions were appointed, one in 1882 and one in 1896. Their major recommendations were to diversify crops, particularly fruit, because the sugar trade was in decline as the competition of sugar beet was too strong.

The man most prominently identified with the movement to develop the region's economic and agricultural resources was Sir Daniel Morris. In 1879 he was appointed Director of Public Gardens and Plantations in Jamaica and in 1884 proposed to the Royal Commission, set up to enquire into the economic circumstances of the West Indies, that a network of small botanic gardens or stations should be set up through out the Caribbean. They should have the specific task of carrying out trials of new agricultural and horticultural crops which would be suitable for the particular climate and soils of each island. Although they were to carry out this task effectively, the gardens were also very quickly to become quasi-public parks growing a wide variety of ornamental plants and developing layouts which would encourage visitors not only to learn but also to enjoy their pleasant environments. The idea was accepted and with the active assistance of the Royal Botanic Gardens, Kew (of which Morris had just been appointed Assistant Director) botanic gardens or stations were established in the following islands: Barbados, Grenada, Antigua, St Vincent (where the old botanic garden was to be revived), St Lucia, St Kitts and Nevis, Montserrat and Dominica. The Virgin Islands were omitted from the list at that stage on the grounds that their economy could not support the required expenditure although, in fact, a botanic station was established later.

19

Morris's continued commitment to the Caribbean was demonstrated when he took up the appointment of Imperial Commissioner of Agriculture for the West Indies. In this position he pioneered the extension of lime and cacao culture and he also re-introduced Sea Island cotton before his retirement in 1908.

Morris also pioneered the introduction of new sugar-cane hybrids which had been bred to give both a higher sucrose content and greater resistance to disease. These, together with a wider use of fertilisers and the introduction of the ridge method of planting (which prevented flooding after heavy rain) ensured the renewed success of the Caribbean sugar crop.

The historian, J A Froude, has left an evocative account of the garden of the Residency on Dominica at that time:

A broad walk with clipped limes on one side, and a lawn dotted with oleanders and hibiscus on the other, led to the main door. Lizards basked on the stone steps and stephanotis shrouded the iron railings with its perfumed blooms.

The sweet-scented oleander flowers add pleasure when the plant is used as hedging.

In 1902 an annual Arbor Day was inaugurated in the British islands as a way of encouraging tree-planting. Every year thereafter on the King's birthday, the Governors of the West Indies would inaugurate the day with a ceremonial tree-planting in Government House gardens or elsewhere in their jurisdiction. The planting of commemorative trees had by that time become quite common. The earliest recorded was the Norfolk Island pine planted by Prince Albert, later Duke of Edinburgh, when he was guest of Sir Graham Biggs at Farley Hill on Barbados in 1861. Archdeacon Brindley, Principal of Codrington College, also on Barbados, recorded the planting of two cabbage palms, one by Prince George (later George V) and the other by Prince Edward when they visited from their ship in 1879. The one planted by Prince Edward died. When in 1892, the news of the prince's death arrived, the Archdeacon related how the people who worked at the college were not at all surprised: 'We know Prince Eddy die soon,' was their suspicious lament, 'his cabbage die'. At Prospect Plantation in Jamaica trees can be seen which were planted by Sir Winston Churchill, Henry Kissinger, Charlie Chaplin, Pierre Trudeau and Sir Noel Coward, to name but a few. Some individual trees have more than purely ornamental significance, for example, the great banyan tree in front of the King's House in Jamaica in the roots of which it is said the *duppies* (as ghosts are called in Jamaica) take refuge when they are not in the silk cotton trees, or the tree called the Signature Tree, an ancient yucca located on the island of Anguilla which marks a water-filled cavern known as the Fountain, from which during times of drought the islanders could fill their buckets.

After the First World War, the Caribbean's healthy winter climate and elegant plantation houses began to attract a new group of wealthy residents from Europe and the United States, many of whom were keen gardeners. Some built new houses and laid out new gardens. The tradition of making grand, formal private gardens had not been entirely lost during the economic depression of the late nineteenth century. The elaborate cast-iron fountains and balustraded terraces of the gardens of Government House, St John (laid out between 1865 and 1887) and of the gardens of Devon House, Kingston, Jamaica (laid out in 1881 by George Stiebel, one of the first black millionaires in the Caribbean) testify to that. The gardens of the 1930s were, however, laid out in a more eclectic, sophisticated mixture of materials and styles. At Glitter Bay in Barbados, Sir Edward Cunard built a house of coral rock which was surrounded by tree-shaded vistas edged with pillared urns, cupid-crowned gate-piers and a beach pavilion modelled on the Renaissance pavilion of the Villa Caprarola in Italy. Francia Plantation's house and garden were also modelled on Italian Renaissance examples. Tower House in Grenada was built of dark volcanic rock in a mixture of English Renaissance and Baroque styles, but its garden was given a 'modern' aspect by the use of the 'new' material, concrete, for the construction of its garden walls and ornamental niches. Concrete was also used in the reconstruction of the house and garden at the Habitation Ceron in Martinique.

James Pope-Hennessy in his book *West Indian Summer* [1943] gives a composite picture of the gardens at Government House, Port of Spain in Trinidad; the white-painted house and garden walls, the white-uniformed staff, the polished brass cannon by the portico and tubs of crotons by the door. Stephanotis curled around the ironwork of the verandas, a formal flower garden with a white-painted urn was also planted with crotons and tree-shaded lawns were edged with tall saman trees and royal palms. Using the pseudonym 'Cashel' he also evokes a vivid picture of the gardens at Government House on Barbados as they appeared to him on his first visit to the tropics:

There in the long walled garden of another Government House grew cannon-ball trees and calabash trees, cabbage palms, and cluster upon cluster of bamboo. The trees threw heavy shadows across the lawns and pathways, over the beds of red and blue

The cannonball tree may be interesting to look at but the opened flower has an evil smell.

flowers, over the negro gardeners in their white cotton coats. As he gazed upon this garden, Cashel realised how the Victorian interest in the odd and excessive found its ideal in tropical foliage. He understood the vogue of the conservatory and the glasshouse. It was easy to picture English visitors of the 'fifties strolling entranced around this very garden, wondering idly at much their pale Barbadian hosts would take for granted – the cabbage palms towering above, the calabash and trumpet trees, the giant canna blossoms, the brilliance of bougainvillea seen at last in its proper setting, the white stephanotis against the blood-red hibiscus hedge, the swish of the hummingbirds darting, the long, long ropes of creeper looped wildly about the high trees. All around them would echo the shrill sad repetition of tropical birds' cries, and towards evening the fireflies, those nightly miracles, would flash and sparkle over the lawns in the early darkness.

After the Second World War, one final house and garden were made in the grand formal style. The renowned connoisseur, Ronald Tree, employed the great English landscape architect, Sir Geoffrey Jellicoe, to design a house and garden at Sandy Lane on Barbados which was in the Italian Palladian Style. Air travel was making the Caribbean accessible as a winter resort for larger numbers of people. In the 1950s and 1960s, Mr Tree developed the land around Sandy Lane as a luxurious holiday complex bringing Richard Coghlan, a graduate of the Royal Botanic Gardens, Kew, from England to supervise the complex's planting. A similar approach to the planning and planting of a holiday resort was adopted by Laurance S. Rockefeller in the creation of the Caneel Bay resort on St John which was opened in 1952. These became the models on which most subsequent landscaping schemes for resort complexes in the Caribbean were based.

It was partly to meet the demand for exotic plants for use in such schemes throughout the Caribbean that Andromeda Gardens in Barbados were founded in the early 1960s by Iris Bannochie. Over a period of about thirty years, she introduced thousands of new species and hybrid plants to Barbados.

However, many of the region's visitors wished to stay, not in some new-built resort, but to sample the elegant way of life of the plantation houses, some of which were now converted into small discreet inns with their old gardens re-vitalised. Outstanding gardens resulting from this kind of restoration include those at the atmospheric Hotel Plantation de Leyritz on Martinique and at the reconstructed Montpelier Plantation Inn on Nevis. Elegant plantation living was also recalled for visitors to the private island of Mustique in the Grenadines when in the 1960s Lord Glenconner, with the assistance of theatrical designer Oliver Messel, developed a 'West Indian Georgian' style of holiday house and garden. A few of the houses on the island had what might be called 'fantasy' gardens – that of Lord Glenconner was created in a Gingerbread-Moghul style, that of David Bowie in a tropical Balinese style, for example. With garden-visiting becoming a popular activity high on the list of many visitors, some old plantation gardens, formerly private, were opened to the public by appointment. Francia Plantation on Barbados and the Tower House on Grenada retain the atmosphere of grand plantation gardens and both are beautifully planted and well maintained.

New gardens were also created in response to the demands of tourism. The botanical gardens in St Thomas, St Croix and the Bay Gardens in Grenada are good examples. These are not botanical gardens in the strictest sense in that they do not carry out any substantial botanical research. Nor are they botanical gardens in the sense that the older botanical gardens of the Caribbean were so described as being places primarily for the introduction of new useful and commercial plants. These new 'botanical' gardens are called botanical by reason of the large number and variety of ornamental plants which are growing in them, designed to display to the casual visitor the abundance and richness of nature in the tropics and to educate the house-owner in the Caribbean about plants which may be suitable for him or her to grow in their own gardens. Three magnificent new 'display' gardens of this kind have been established in the last decade. Le Jardin de Balata in Martinique was begun by the French artist Jean-Philippe Thoze in 1982 and opened to the public in 1986. Already it has earned a place as one of the most beautiful tropical gardens in the world and continues to surprise connoisseurs with its new landscaping ideas. The Joseph Reynold O'Neal Botanic Gardens on Tortola was opened to the public in 1987. It brings to the Caribbean for the first time the ideas of the English compartmented garden, its tropical plants being arranged in a series of connecting outdoor 'rooms' and 'passages'. The Flower Forest in Barbados has been planted by Richard Coghlan, author of the book *Landscaping in the Tropics*, as a kind of natural tropical forest which is filled with flowers throughout the year.

For the garden-lover who finds him- or herself in the Caribbean but out of reach of one of the gardens open to the public, there are often activities associated in one way or another with gardening which are available. Many of the commercial cut-flower nurseries like Macintosh on Martinique or the Mount William Plantation on St Vincent welcome visitors. In these you can enjoy the sight of acres of brilliantly coloured anthuriums, strelitzias and other flowers growing in huge shade-houses. There are also a number of interesting conventional nurseries and garden centres – that of John Criswick at St Rose in Grenada is a source of many rare and unusual plants which are distributed by him throughout the Caribbean. In the early part of each year the Barbados Horticultural Society (one of a number of horticultural societies in the region) organises visits to private gardens. The various National Trusts, like those of Barbados, Montserrat or the British Virgin Islands also organise similar events. Almost every island is now aware of the need for conservation and has established National Park Areas where bromeliads and epiphytes flower in the rainforests and frangipani in the coastal scrub. The mountains are brightened with the red blossoms of African tulip and orange immortelle and tropical water hyacinths flower in the ponds. The joy of discovering plants that flower in the wild is almost as great as seeing them in the garden.

One of the many examples of the bromeliads that grow in the Caribbean islands.

When Sir Daniel Morris lectured to the Horticultural Club in London in 1891 on the subject of gardening in the Caribbean, he described its advantages and disadvantages:

In point of scenery and displays of tropical vegetation, the islands of the Caribbean are among the most beautiful areas in the world. Their inherent fertility and their advantageous geographical position have at various times in history brought them great prosperity. They were once renowned for sugar, supplying close to the entire world's requirement for the crop. Later they became renowned for fruit, spices and other agricultural crops.

When there are so many conditions favourable to the growth of plants, the task of the cultivator is to repress rather than to urge. He has to fight against tropical weeds with a persistency his northern brother can scarcely realise. Heavy downpours of rain and the fierce rays of the sun have to be equally borne, hence shrubs and trees are more in favour than herbaceous plants. Indeed delicate plants require the shelter of trees and rocks ...

The long history of gardening in the Caribbean has fluctuated in response to outside events and changing human needs but the climate has remained a constant. In recent years many gardens in the region have been devastated in a series of severe hurricanes yet a garden's recuperative powers in this climate and these soils is astonishing. As a result, gardening in the Caribbean has seldom been in such good heart.

Traveller's tree or traveller's palm (*Ravenala madagascariensis*). (Chris Huxley)

25

 JAMAICA

Introduction and history

In 1509 the Spaniards became the first of the Europeans to settle in Jamaica after Columbus' discovery in the previous century. They did not set great value on the island because they had settled Hispaniola, Cuba and Puerto Rico at the same time, and there appeared to be no gold in Jamaica. There were only a few settlements along the coasts and the land was used for raising cattle to provide meat, tallow and hides to the passing ships and cotton for goods such as hammocks. Cocoa, tobacco and fruit were also grown.

In 1655 an expedition planned by the Commonwealth government of Oliver Cromwell arrived in Barbados and made its way northwards on a recruiting mission, visiting Nevis, St Kitts and Montserrat before attacking Hispaniola. This was a spectacular failure and the English hastily

The French peanut (*Sterculia apetala*) is a native of tropical America.

withdrew and turned their attention to Jamaica. Here they had more success as the Spanish fled over the mountains to the north coast. The badly-led and disorganised English expedition failed to follow up its advantage and the Spaniards provided a disruptive element until the Treaty of Madrid in 1670 recognised England's right of possession. Jamaica remained in English hands until its independence in the twentieth century.

Gardening climate

The mountains of Jamaica account for the island's variations in climate. The misty valleys of the Rio Grande have a lush wet tropical climate while west of Kingston in the Hellshire Hills it is dry enough for cacti to flourish. Within an hour's driving the climate can vary from wet to dry, and the scenery from hot lowlands to cool hill country. The mountain pastures are cool and green. The pattern of rainfall also varies with the season and the prevailing wind. From November to April, when the winds are northeasterly, rainfall is mainly concentrated in the Blue Mountains. From May to October, when winds tend to be more easterly, rainfall is concentrated along the higher land across the island.

Altitude also has an influence on temperature. The higher up, the cooler the temperature. At sea-level, the night temperature seldom falls below 20°C, but above 5000 feet there can very occasionally be frost.

Days are shorter in December, and some plants, for example the poinsettia, have adapted, blooming with the shortening day.

Gardening soils

Jamaica is the top of a drowned mountain range, the highest peak of which, Blue Mountain Peak, would be almost as high as Everest if the sea were drained away. The land sweeps upwards swiftly and the mountains account for the variations of soil throughout the island. The eastern quarter of Jamaica is the result of volcanic eruptions, terraces and plateaus ranging from 1500 to 3500 feet above sea-level. The thick limestone blanket, which is the parent rock of most of Jamaica, influences the soils of the island. Most Caribbean soils are formed as a result of leaching where the water, moving downwards through the soil drains away into rivers, resulting in the loss of minerals. The bauxite for which Jamaica is famous was left in the 'red earth' along with iron. The soils on the plateaus tend to be thin, dark rendzinas, made from decayed plants mixed in with weathered limestone, with lots of animal activity, particularly from earthworms. The soils on the slopes tend to be the thinnest, because of gravity, especially where the forest cover has been removed, leaving the soil exposed to erosion. This soil has sometimes gathered in the foothills, where it may be quite thick.

Gardening history

In 1687 the Duke of Albermarle arrived in Jamaica with his physician, Sir Hans Sloane. Most of the island was uninhabited at this time. Sir Hans published a detailed description of Jamaica and its plants. His collections are in the Natural History Museum, London. On his return to London, he bought the land of the Society of Apothecaries' garden, where he had been a student. The Chelsea Physic Garden was established on the site. In his account of Jamaica Sir Hans described the many Indians, saying that they originated from Florida and the Mosquito Cays (off South America) as the original inhabitants had been killed off by the Spaniards. By 1688 there were also many negroes, brought in by the slave traders – sugar had been cultivated for some time. He made the doctor's observation that those negroes who were born in Jamaica were healthier than those brought from Africa.

The Spaniards had imported many plants from South America which had naturalised prolifically. The land was very fertile, there were many rivers, some very swift, as well as salt ponds. The growth was so lush that abandoned plantations soon became overgrown. There the usual diet was salt meat and fresh beef was available, although when the animal was slaughtered in the early morning the meat had to be eaten that day, otherwise it went putrid. There were also pigs which lived in the woods and came to the call of a conchshell when blown. Poultry, turkeys and Muscovy ducks (from Guinea) were raised for eating as well. Manatees (sea cows) were eaten by the Indians and turtles were caught off the Cayman Islands and south

A corner of Shaw Gardens where many layers of vegetation flourish in the fertile soil.

islands of Cuba by a fleet of 180 sloops of the Port Royal fleet. Potatoes, yams, maize, rice, cassava and plantains were all grown. Cassava loaves were used instead of bread because there was a great problem with weevils in imported flour. Chocolate was a very popular drink and widely used, being beaten up with eggs which Sloane said was not good for people (too rich presumably) but a lot of water was drunk which was regarded as healthy.

The Spaniards had built low thatched houses of clay on reeds which survived earthquakes satisfactorily whereas the English built in brick which was declared not to be as good or as cool. Hammocks draped with mosquito nets were used by almost everyone. Burials had to be quick and, as a result, there were graveyards on the plantations. The local horses were very small and swift but with little stamina. They were a Spanish breed and there were many roaming wild in the woods, as well as wild cattle. By this time the range of exports was excellent – sugar, indigo, cotton, ginger, allspice, fustick wood, 'princewood', lignum vitae, sarsaparilla, cocoa and cochineal.

As can be seen from the list above, farming in Jamaica was not a monoculture as found in some of the other islands. Sugar had been grown from the middle years of the seventeenth century, so the social upheaval wrought by the slave trade did not have the same effect in Jamaica as in some of the other islands, although it did become the most profitable sugar island in the eighteenth century.

The estates were bigger in Jamaica than in the smaller islands. It was during this century that most of the great houses were built, most as centres for their plantations, and gardens were laid out. It was also at this time that so

many handsome public buildings were erected. There was a garrison at Jamaica and a naval base, both of which meant the building of barracks, accommodation and all the necessary outbuildings. Settlers moved out into the countryside so it was no longer an island with only small settlements round its coasts. The great houses were very beautifully ornamented with the handsome local woods used for their doors, windows and staircases as well as for furniture. Jamaica, however, escaped the destruction of the wars that was wreaked on some of the other islands. She went on producing sugar and between 1748–56 the prices rose. There was a boom because England was in command of the Caribbean, many of the French islands having been captured.

When, further south in St Vincent, the first botanic garden in the western hemisphere was started in 1765 Edward Long, Speaker of the House of Assembly, in his *History of Jamaica* of 1774, expressed surprise that the gentlemen of Jamaica had allowed St Vincent to be ahead of them in the matter of starting a botanic garden.

The first move in Jamaica came when a piece of land called Enfield was purchased by the government prior to the appointment and arrival in 1775 of Dr Thomas Clarke as the island's first botanist. Appropriate plants were also imported for a European and tropical garden. However the land was considered too steep for a botanical garden. Meanwhile Mr Hinton East, who was an attorney and civil servant, had started a garden in 1776 on his own property in a lower area known as Liguanea. This was next to Enfield, near Gordon Town, St Andrew, and he called it Spring Garden. In his *Hortus Eastensis* which was published in 1792, Hinton East lists his acquisitions which he reckoned to be some of the earliest introductions: cupressus, mulberry, tulip tree, cassia, casuarina, magnolia, bauhinia, hibiscus, oleander, azalea, cork oak, rhododendron, jasmine and temperate plants such as watercress and geranium. He comments that the date palm had probably been brought in by Jews who came from Portugal in the early sixteenth century.

Because of the unsuitability of Enfield another piece of land was acquired by the government, this time at Bath, 28 miles east of Kingston. Even this was a poor choice as, though the climate was good for tropical plants, the site was liable to flooding from the river nearby and the soil was river wash. Dr Clarke was interested in medical and scientific plants and his acquisitions reflected this: teas, camphor, litchee, cycad, jujube, clove, dracaena, dye plants, and plants producing resins, varnishes and cabinet woods. One of the beneficial effects of the war with the French was the capture of one of their ships in 1782 with a cargo of plants on its way to Haiti from Mauritius. The spice plants on board were destroyed by the French captain who regarded them as too valuable to fall into British hands, but the rest were divided between Bath and Mr East's garden, his garden still being highly regarded and Bath not always well maintained. But cinnamon, jak fruit, pandanus, moringa and ebony were acquired. At much the same time as this Mauritius was taken by the British from the French.

Lord Rodney, the English Admiral, ordered some young mango trees to be taken to Jamaica. The mango originated in South-East Asia and was to prove prolific in the

The cycads are purported to be one of the oldest plant forms on Earth.

Caribbean. By 1784 the trees were doing well and fruiting. In a letter from Mr East to Sir Joseph Banks in London he mentions the desirability of importing breadfruit from the Pacific as an additional food for the slaves. The slaves ate a lot of plantain at this period.

Mr East was in frequent correspondence with both Sir Joseph Banks and Kew Gardens, sending parcels of Jamaican plants to them in return for those he received. He died in 1792 and his nephew sold Spring Garden to the government. At this time it had an area of 193 acres and was sold with its buildings and slaves. It was nearer the capital than Bath and, although the river ran near, it was less liable to flooding. It now became known as the Botanic Garden, Liguanea.

In 1793 Captain Bligh and his cargo of breadfruit from the Pacific arrived at Port Royal on the ship *Providence*. This was his second and successful attempt to transport it, the first having ended in the infamous mutiny on his ship the *Bounty*. The cargo was divided between the Bath nursery and Liguanea, and the Parishes of the Three Counties. James Wiles had been chosen by Banks to go to the Pacific and bring back the breadfruit plants. He stayed on in Jamaica at Bath and the next year was put in charge of Liguanea as well. Wiles lived on in Jamaica to be quite an old man, became a planter and kept up his friendship with Matthew Flinders who had been on the famous voyage with him. He declared the breadfruit from that voyage not to have been a great success but this may have been because at first the slaves would not eat it. The mango he said was a great success.

All during these years, 1788 to 1803, and the various hostilities, amicable exchanges of plants were going on between French Haiti and Jamaica – surprising to modern thinking but pleasant. By 1810 Jamaica was going through hard times and the planters, all members of the House of Assembly, felt Liguanea was not worth the money being spent on it. (James Wiles was still there as superintendent.) It was decided to sell and the For Sale notice gave an acreage of 94 acres on the banks of the Hope River. A Dr Gordon bought it but the garden was in decline; by 1843 it was referred to as the 'old Botanic Garden' and was a complete wilderness, with only a few of its large trees left. It had earned a mention in Loudon's *Encyclopedia of Gardening* in 1824 where he gave the acreage and the story of the French ship but added to the list of plants mangosteen, star apple, gum arabic and sassafras. Loudon deplored the fact that the government sold it for a mere £4,000. In the 1835 edition of his *Encyclopedia* he says that the Jamaica Society for the Encouragement of Arts and Agriculture *gave premiums for the raising of horticultural productions both to free persons and to slaves but none of the ornamental departments of gardening are at all attended to by this society.* In a still later edition Loudon mentions Bath as being the botanic garden of Jamaica. It had fluctuating fortunes being nearly abandoned for want of funds but, in 1848, Nathaniel Wilson became curator. He was regarded as probably the best of all curators and Bath performed the duties of a botanic garden providing planters and farmers with new and useful species. Loudon added again to the list of plants, for instance the gamboge tree, the wax palm, new fruits of the granadilla kind (*Passiflora edulis*, *P. incarnata*) and mandarin oranges. In 1858 there was an exceptionally bad flood at Bath and part of the garden was ruined. It was decided the garden was too small anyway – it was laid out in a square with a surrounding path like so many of the old geometrically shaped gardens – and on 29th November 1863 Castleton garden was established at a

height of 500 feet. It had a rainfall of 115 inches a year. There was also criticism about this site having a river running through it because it could flood too. At 19 miles from Kingston it was still thought too far. In spite of local niggardliness the garden became very rich in plants due to Nathaniel Wilson and Dr Hooker of Kew, who in 1869 sent 400 specimens with a horticulturist. Many plants were also sent over from Bath. Marianne North, the Victorian lady painter who travelled so widely and intrepidly all over the world, has left a description of Bath and the gardens in 1871. *The old botanical garden had long since been left to the care of nature but to my mind no gardener could have treated it better, for everything grew as it liked and the ugly formal paths were almost undiscoverable. The most gorgeous trees were tangled up with splendid climbing plants all seeding and flowering luxuriantly, the yellow fruit of the gamboge strewed the ground under them and the screw pine rested on its stilted roots, over which hoya plants were twining, covered with their sweet star flowers.*

In 1868 it was decided to try growing tea and cinchona, the bark of which provides the anti-malarial drug quinine. For this purpose Hill Garden or, as it became known, Cinchona, was founded. These gardens were 4–5000 feet up on a ridge with magnificent views of Strawberry Hill, Green River, the Blue Mountains and Kingston. The idea was that the site was particularly suitable for plants which like a cool climate. Forty acres was put to cinchona, Assam tea was grown and there was an area for European plants.

The sealing wax palm is a particularly decorative member of the palm family.

The cinchona grew well and the gardens became the head-quarters of the department for public gardens. By 1881, 250 acres of cinchona were established in the garden and planters were also growing it.

However Cinchona, or Hill Gardens, represented a lost opportunity by the government. They did not wish to spend money on it, or on the roads which would have connected it to the local market, or to factories that would have processed the tea and cinchona. They decided the competition from India was overwhelming and there was not enough labour for tea-picking. The European garden was more successful and introduced vegetables and flowers sold readily in the Kingston market. The agriculturists felt there were great possibilities for future prosperity based on growing vegetables and many imported vegetables and fruit would grow well there, but once again the opportunity was ignored.

Concern was being felt in Britain at this time about the state of the West Indian islands. Their economies were debt-ridden and their land suffered from the inclination to monoculture of sugar, which impoverishes the land. Two Royal Commissions were appointed, one in 1882 and one in 1896. In 1879 Dr Daniel Morris had been appointed as Director of Public Gardens and Plantations in Jamaica and he wrote a paper, *Planting Enterprises in the West Indies* which was presented to the British Parliament, and must have been one of the stimulants for the Royal Commission. As a direct result of the Commission a system of botanical gardens was set up throughout the British West Indies, with the intention of introducing new crops, distributing seeds and plants to the planters and instructing the youth in modern farming methods. Jamaica had already being doing some of this work, as had Barbados.

Whatever the view of the authorities in Britain or the West Indies to newcomers, the growth of plants and their diversity were remarkable in the islands. A private party in a large yacht visited various islands in 1884/5 and Lady Brassey, wife of the owner, has left a lively and well-informed account of what she saw. She does not appear to have been very impressed by Kingston and Port Royal but there was a small garden known as the Parade Garden in Kingston which had lovely orchids, pink water lilies and *the sacred bean of India* (presumably she meant the lotus). The road of Liguanea had hedges of cactus, *dagger plants*, jasmine, blue and scarlet convolvuli, poinsettia, bois immortelle, scarlet and yellow flamboyant and allamanda in great profusion and confusion. Around the house where the party stayed the growth was just as prolific. She noted mango trees, stephanotis, clerodendron, bauhinia, roses and tuberoses. A large ackee tree gave shade in the garden and there were mimosa, magnolia and star apple. There were also pineapples, orchids and bromeliads. In the custom of the day they got up very early – at five a.m. – for the start of any expeditions they took. She went out to the botanical garden at Gordon Town nine miles north-east of Kingston where the Hope river was in spate. On the way she noted the large tamarind, silk cotton, ackee trees and daturas in the gardens. What fascinated her was how everything seemed to grow, both from temperate climes like roses, carnations and lilies and from the tropics like allamanda, stephanotis, caladium, croton, dracaena, litchi, mango, bois immortelle and orchids.

Many different orchids will grow in Caribbean gardens. These plants have been naturalised in a tree.

The party also visited Newcastle, at that time a garrison outpost and a place where the troops could recover from any illnesses caught on the plain. On the way up she noted ginger and lemon grass, growing wild, plus tree ferns and many British wild flowers. They passed coffee estates and plantations of cinchona. She relates that different types of cinchona were grown at different altitudes and that dracaena was used to mark the boundary lines of estates.

Another expedition was to Fern Walk, presumably the place now referred to as Fern Gully, where she saw tree ferns and orchids draping the trees and the fruit-bearing tree, the genip. The wonderful lushness of the growth impressed her once more. *In every available nook and cranny were pretty little cottages … surrounded by large gardens planted with fruit bearing trees … breadfruit, coconut, ackee, mango, citron, orange and pomelos.* They crossed over the island and on the north coast found the orange harvest being collected. Each fruit was wrapped in a maize leaf to be packed for export. She observed more orchids and said there were many, many large orange trees and plenty of cattle on that coast and also pimento trees.

Dr Daniel Morris, having served some years in Jamaica, returned to England and Kew, but in 1890 it was decided he should undertake a tour of inspection in the West Indies to report on the progress of the various botanical stations and gardens that had been established or were to be established as a result of the Royal Commission. When he got to Jamaica he mentioned the laying out of the Hope Gardens. This time roads and drives were laid with plans for ornamental planting, but it was also to have an experimental facility and a research department. An industrial school was established and attached to the Hope Garden where boys attended daily and observed practical demonstrations in agriculture. As part of the encouragement to better efforts it was suggested that agricultural exhibitions and shows should be held; there was one in Jamaica at this time.

The *Gardener's Chronicle* of February 1896 published an extract from a book *A Collecting Tour of Jamaica* by W Harris which gave the following account: *We also passed thriving plantations of Chocolate and nutmegs growing under the shade of bananas. Here we noticed also a number of large trees of* Eugenia malaccensis *and* Barringtonia speciosa *and many other trees spread from the old botanic garden in Bath. There is now only a remnant of the old garden, only about one acre in extent it contains fine specimens of* Barringtonia speciosa, Spathodia campanulata, Lagerstroemia flosreginae, Cinnamomum zeylanicum, Myristica fragrans, … Napoleona imperialis, *etc … It was simply a jungle until two years ago when a good deal of necessary pruning and thinning were done … to give more light and air … trees and plants labelled with neat enamelled iron labels. The place was put in good order, benches provided, walks laid out … and order restored. Bath is an ideal place for a botanic garden – a warm humid atmosphere, frequent showers and good soil but the distance from the capital is against it.*

It is the sadder after all this enthusiasm to read of the hurricane in 1903. Once again the *Gardener's Chronicle* reported: *All the public gardens are situated on the eastern end of the island, they have all been much damaged. The one that suffered most the Hill Gardens, situated on the Blue Mountains. At Hill Garden nearly every large tree has been blown down, the Tree ferns de-stemmed. At the Hope Garden all the great Saman and other trees are on the ground. The Castleton Gardens have been wrecked by hurricanes three times in the last twenty-three years. Gangs are now busy with axes, cutlasses and saws cutting up trees that a few days ago were the glory of our public gardens. The careful labour of years was practically wiped out in a couple of hours.* This account illustrates the sadness of gardening in the West Indies; the hurricanes can be very frequent and violent, although regrowth is also fast.

At time of writing Hope Gardens is still going and a new lease of life is planned for it and for its continuation with its experimental and scientific work. Hill Garden still exists and still has its plantations, but Bath is fading away.

A breadfruit tree, the acquisition of which was main purpose of Captain Bligh's voyages to the Caribbean and the Pacific. The notice commemorates this.

Castleton exists and is still cared for. It would be a wonderful thing if more money could be devoted to these lost glories, particularly in view of the modern research into the uses, medicinal and otherwise, of plants as well as concern felt over disappearing species.

Gardens

 BARBICAN GARDENS
BOONE HALL, STONY HILL

This is a plant nursery and restaurant owned by Mr Stephen Jones. It was a farm of ten acres when he bought it, on a steeply sloping hillside with a river running at the bottom of the valley. When the river is full it adds a very attractive feature to the site. Mr Jones has been in business for fourteen years as a plantsman and the pleasant site gave him the idea for the restaurant. The plants that are being grown are fairly common ones for gardens in the Caribbean climate. There are two large shade houses for house plants. He has a lot of his stock in the ground and much of propagating is done on the place by cuttings and by using the foil method, i.e. scraping the bark and wrapping the area in moist peat then wrapping it in foil. In the shade houses there are many hanging baskets full of such plants as ivies and small philodendrons. There are

One of the happy occupants of Barbican Gardens.

containers of dieffenbachia, anthuriums and palms of different kinds. He seems to have a preference for plants with white variegated leaves and for white anthuriums but these, of course, would lighten a dark corner or an interior. There are large trees up the hillside giving the shade that is needed, a left-over from the farm. A very big star apple (*Chrysophyllum cainito*) is one which is unusual and there are citrus plus bananas, torch lilies (*Etlingera elatior*), heliconias and crotons with an underplanting of pink and white begonias. Busy hens make their way through all this.

Restaurant   Owner Mr Stephen Jones,
Telephone: 977-0033

✑ CASTLETON BOTANIC GARDENS ✑
WAG WATER GORGE, JUNCTION ROAD

Castleton Gardens were established in 1862 as a successor to the Bath Gardens and many of the original plants were sent over from Bath to establish Castleton. The garden was laid out by Nathaniel Wilson who was regarded as probably the greatest curator of gardens Jamaica ever had. He corresponded with Dr Hooker of Kew who in 1869 sent out 400 specimen plants and a horticulturist, Mr Thompson, to assist. The garden was laid out on sandy loam on a sloping site in the Wag Water Gorge with the river running through the garden and the road dividing

The palm collection at Castleton Botanic Gardens.

it. There was still a problem of flooding at times from the river, a problem that had prompted the move from Bath, but the garden thrived and became very rich in plants. Today there are still many remarkable specimens.

The upper part of the garden was used for a palmetum, a fernery, a formal garden and an arboretum, the lower section between the river and the road was designated for economic plants and experimental cultivation. The most striking feature of the upper garden today is the large sloping green lawn with the palms planted there. The *Araucaria cunninghamii* and *A. excelsa* are part of the original planting. By 1897 there were 180 palm species in the garden although there are not so many today. There are the straw palm which gives jippi jappa straw used in hats (*Raphia farinifera*), the betel nut palm (*Areca catechu*), the lady finger palm (*Rhapis excelsa*), the Japanese fan palm (*Pritchardia pacifica*), a huge talipot palm (*Corypha umbraculifera*), the dwarf date palm (*Phoenix roebelinii*), the Alexander palm, the bull thatch palm (*Sabal maritima*), a native, the fishtail palm (*Caryota mitis*), the queen palm (*Syagrus romanzoffiana*), the royal palm (*Roystonea regia*) from Cuba, the sugar palm from which is made palm wine and saccharine (*Arenga saccharifera*). There is also a large clump of bamboo – *Melocanna* – which provide good furniture wood as it is termite resistant.

Paths wind away up and down the hill, forming a circuitous route. Along these are all sorts of interesting plants. Heliconias grow on the edge of the paths in the shade of trees such as a guango (*Samanea saman*) and a *Brownea grandiceps*. There is the *Michelia champaca* from Asia with its perfumed bark, a black ebony from which piano keys are made, the *Diospyros discolor* or velvet apple and a camphor tree. Underplanted is *Miconia magnifica*, another native, with its unusual leaf – green and white on top, red on the underside. A cannonball tree (*Couroupita guianensis*) stands slightly apart with its unusual form of growth, the flowers coming directly from the lower trunk

and the leaves on the upper branches. There are several ferns in the underplanting, one an iridescent fern which marks the skin when pressed against it, and a giant Australian fern as well as the plant known as the hummingbird fountain from the water held in its leaves (*Sanchezia nobilis*) a native of Ecuador. Groups of cycads stand in grassy areas and orchids and bromeliads cling and climb up the bigger trees. Shell ginger also grows in the partial shade. There is a rambutan and a mangosteen tree and also a strychnine tree (*Strychnos nux-vomica*). The bark of the strychnine is an antidote for its poisonous berries. There is an ochna with yellow flowers very like those of yellow allamanda and an iron wood tree (*Mesua ferrea*) which has very heavy but unsinkable timber. It is also perfumed so is used for bridal beds in India. Near the gate is the Asian *Butea frondosa* which is rare (but there is one in Hope Gardens too) and Napoleon's hat (*Napoleona imperialis*) with its pink blossoms which makes a small attractive tree. The handsome *Amherstia nobilis* is here and three differently scented pimentos – bay rum, lemon and allspice. A lovely vine with long red racemes (*Norantea guianensis*), the extraordinary jade vine (*Strongylodon macrobotrys*) with its jade-green flowers and *Thunbergia mysorensis* with red and yellow flowers all grow in this area.

The arboretum is in the upper eastern section of the garden and here are more large trees such as *Gynocardia odorata* which is tall and resinous and comes from Sikkim and the padauk (*Pterocarpus indicus*) which is a good shade tree and flowers in the time of the monsoon in India. The bullet tree – balata (*Manilkara bidentata*) is from Surinam and produces a kind of gutta-percha, a hard, rubber-like

The unusually coloured flowers of the jade vine make it a point of interest everywhere it grows.

substance at one time used in golf balls. There is also a collection of dracaenas.

The lower garden was for economic plants and *Tabebuia pallida* is used as a shade tree. The *Brownea grandiceps* from South America is here (its common name is rose of Venezuela) as is the dammar pine (*Agathis orientalis*) which is one of the world's tallest trees. It gives gum copal which is a very good quality varnish. There is also a large guango (*Samanea saman*).

At one time this area was a coffee plantation; *Coffea liberica* proved to be the hardiest coffee as *C. arabica* got

various diseases, and *C. robusta* was grown too. The African tulip tree (*Spathodea campanulata*) is often seen in Jamaica, in fact it seems to have naturalised for one often sees the brilliant red blossoms in the bush on the roadside. The Burma teak (*Tectona grandis*) was tried here and has proved very successful in Trinidad. Mahogany (*Swietenia mahagoni*) is much slower growing and takes 80 years to grow to a useful size. The immortelles (*Erythina pallida* and *E. umbrosa*) are used for shading young cocoa trees and the poison can be used for stunning fish.

This garden is used as a park by local people but it is still probably the best cared for public garden in Jamaica, owing to its 11 gardeners and the attentions of Mr Roy Bennett who shows people around the place that he has loved all his life. Of course it could do with more money and some of the valuable plants being replaced, but it is still a wonderful garden.

Gardens open daily 7.00 am to 6.00 pm
Telephone: 927–1257

SHAW PARK
OCHO RIOS

Shaw Park is a favourite stop on the tourist route and there are plenty of guides who wish to show you round the gardens. However, if by this time you know some of your tropical plants, a walk on your own is more peaceful. It is a

The fallen African tulip tree makes a dramatic bridge over the pond.

garden laid out on a hillside with a beautiful river tumbling down through it. From the car-park and the upper area with its big lawn and small summer house long flights of steps lead down. Some of these have pergolas laden with bougainvillea. Half-way down is a pleasant viewing spot where the river flows over a huge rock and stands of heliconias and crotons grow on the bank. There are several bridges over the river where the path winds back and forth. Big trees such as mahoe (*Hibiscus elatus*) and *Samanea saman* give shade. Planted below them are banks of begonias and more heliconias. There are several streams, smaller waterfalls and little viewing houses. Along these paths are a collection of different coloured hibiscus, crotons and acalypha. A walk-way lined with palms (*Veitchia merrillii*) in the valley leads to a big pool with a huge *Ficus benghalensis* near by. A large African tulip tree (*Spathodea campanulata*) has fallen over the pool providing a romantic bridge above the water lilies. There are some very lush bamboo round the edges of the garden and some big spathodeas. As one climbs back up the hill the fencing by the path is draped in Barbados flower fence (*Caesalpinia pulcherrima*) and yellow *Allamanda cathartica*.

Gardens open daily 9.00 am to 5.00 pm.
Telephone: 974–8888

Coyaba
OCHO RIOS, ST ANN

On the same hillside as Shaw Park Gardens and reached by the same entrance road, is a new garden called Coyaba. It is hard to believe that this garden has been achieved in such a short space of time so lush is the growth, so established does it feel and look. The land was bought about 1990. Three and a half years were spent in planning and it has been open two years. The owner, Mr Stewart, was prompted entirely out of a love for gardens and nature. His ideas have been helped enormously by the fact that there were already many large trees on the site, some ruins and a stream. The stream comes from a locally well-known mineral spring. It is especially good water and contains both zinc and calcium. There is an unusual mixture of soils in the garden, alkaline in places, patches of acid soil and even clay as well. A gardener's dream! There is a particular emphasis on local plants and all are locally grown. There is much interesting work going on behind the scenes as Mr Stewart is in the process of developing a new palm from a *Roystonea* spp. (the royal palm).

The entrance to the garden and the car-park are dominated by a very large native cedar (*Cedrela odorata*) and there are more scattered through the garden, giving the necessary shade for some of the plants. The layout of the garden consists of a circular walk beside the stream which has been guided into a series of pools linked by closely planted stretches. There are little stone bridges crossing at

The stream is a pleasantly cooling feature of Coyaba Gardens.

intervals. Many orchids have been placed on the trees and there are many in the surrounding woodland. One of them is a naturalised vanda which particularly appreciates the coolness.

There are large jasmine bushes (*Jasminum officinale*) and the pink and red ginger (*Alpinia purpurata*). Beside the stream there are many ferns and a spectacular mussaenda bush with peach coloured flowers. This shrub has become very popular in Jamaica and does well. It is originally a native of East Africa.

From Castleton Botanic Garden has come a beeswax heliconia with yellow flowers. Then there is the pinander palm which was developed in Trinidad from the Caribbean royal palm and the solitaire palm (*Ptychosperma elegans*).

Down in a corner of the garden near the shop and little restaurant is a variegated banyan (*Ficus benghalensis*), now a small tree. Eventually this will become so enormous other plants will probably have to come out. Here too are stands of shell ginger, the chenille plant (*Acalypha hispida*) and the *Heliconia psittacorum* with its yellow flowers. Variegated ginger is there too (*Alpinia variegata*) and the torch ginger (*Etlingera elatior*) with its elaborate pink flowers. The latter originally came from the Far East. A calabash tree (*Crescentia cujete*) is also growing well. The underplanting throughout the garden consists of white begonias edging some of the pools, pilea and small dieffenbachias in places.

This is a garden on the tourist circuit and is used for entertaining in the evening and other events but it is tended carefully and with quiet skill by its head gardener,

The magnificent flower of the torch ginger, a plant that likes a shady spot.

Mr Rain Forde who is very knowledgeable. It is open at all the usual times.

Restaurant and shop
Telephone (Mr Rain Forde): 974–6235

❧ DEVON HOUSE ❧
KINGSTON

Devon House was built in the 1880s for a Kingston merchant on Hope Road not far from King's House which was the old Government House and is now the residence of the Governor General. This part of Kingston must have been in the outskirts of the town at the time. The house still has its garden which is entered by large, imposing black wrought-iron gates. The house is built of wood with verandas all round it. It now houses antique and reproduction Jamaican-made furniture and the outbuildings – the old stables and stores – have a shop and restaurant serving Jamaican food. In front of the house is a splendid Victorian fountain and tall royal palms (*Roystonea* spp.) plus some big old mahoganies (*Swietenia mahagoni*) set to frame the view of the front. There are other large and handsome trees such as a boabab (*Adansonia digitata*) near the entrance gates, and a large lignum vitae (*Guaiacum officinale*), possibly as old as the house. On the lawn is a parterre with shrimp plants (*Beloperone guttata*) and the artemisia known as the curry plant. The lily pool in the shape of a shamrock is still there with a small bridge crossing it and there are further lawns but the garden has a lot of public use as a park so naturally there are limitations on its care and maintenance.

Gardens open daily 9.00 am to 5.00 pm.
Restaurant and shop
Telephone: 929–6602

Devon House is one of the finest nineteenth-century houses in the Caribbean.

HOPE BOTANIC GARDENS
KINGSTON

Today Hope Gardens are on the edge of modern-day Kingston, along the Old Hope Road, but in the seventeenth century the land belonged to Richard Hope who had an indigo plantation there that he later adapted to the growing of sugar. During the eighteenth century it was one of the most prosperous sugar estates in the West Indies and 388 slaves worked the plantation. The aqueduct built in 1758, which is still in existence, runs across part of the gardens. It was considered the most up-to-date form of irrigation. In 1874 an experimental station was started on the land and some plants were brought from Castleton. A public park was suggested as well but at that time lack of public transport made this impossible. In 1881 two hundred acres were acquired by the government with the aim of establishing a garden with the climate of the dry south-eastern plain. Fifty acres were devoted to propagation and new varieties of sugar, ten acres were put to teak. Liberian coffee, cacao, and pineapples were planted. Water supply has always been a problem and the remains of efforts to deal with this can be seen in the open lawns of the present-day gardens where small stone-lined runnels still exist. The grass can be very parched at certain times of year. The garden did fulfil its duties as a teaching garden for, in 1897, the *Gardener's Chronicle* noted that *an industrial school has been attached to the Hope Gardens where the boys attend school daily and other times receive practical demonstrations.* Tobacco was also grown and 23 varieties of bananas

45

(some sent from Kew Gardens), coffee, citrus, grape vines and rubber trees.

The fortunes of the gardens have always fluctuated according to the interest of the government of the day. At present, the emphasis is on its use as a public park and large open green space in a sprawling city and there is a zoo attached. The gardens are well cared for in the sense they are clean and tidy but there are no labels on the trees (and the most interesting aspect of the gardens is its collection of large trees). Near the entrance is a moderate sized lake covered with different coloured water lilies. The bridge across is decorated with thunbergia and the South American garlic vine (*Pseudocalymma alliaceum*), both of which have lilac blue flowers. There is also a most striking hedge of cyclamen coloured bougainvillea nearby.

Scattered about the vast lawn beyond the pond are various large trees. Two are of tropical Asian origin – the red cotton tree (*Bombax ceiba*) and the Bengal kino (*Butea monosperma*). The first has scarlet, the second coral-coloured flowers. The French peanut (*Sterculia apetala*), a native of tropical America, has lime-green bell-like flowers hanging in bunches. Beyond this is a thick band of trees and palms with shade-loving plants on either side of the paths that wind through the woodland. There is also, standing free of the woodland, a vast talipot palm (*Corypha umbraculifera*). These large trees take about 60 years to grow to their full size; they then flower with a vast inflorescence carrying 60,000 small white flowers and then they die. There are several of these interesting trees, natives of Ceylon, at various stages of their growth. The palms represented in the band of woodland include the

This tranquil lake is near the entrance and the zoo.

queen palm (*Cocos plumosa*); there are oil palms (*Elaeis guineensis*) as well as the royal palm (*Roystonea*). Beyond this woodland are further great lawns with more large trees, two of which are ant trees or long Johns (*Triplaris americana*) named for the plume-like pink shading to cream bunches of flowers. Flower beds of annuals are on either side of the avenue. The house of the curator and the buildings for the business of the garden are also in this part of the garden.

A turn back towards the entrance leads to an ornamental enclosed garden with annuals, a maze and a shade house with pools of waterplants. There is also a walk entirely covered in flame-coloured bougainvillea, with seats in its shade.

A project has been mooted for the re-establishment of a plant conservation centre at the gardens. A National Arboretum Foundation has been established with the encouragement and help of such prestigious bodies as Kew Gardens, the Fairchild Tropical Garden of Miami, Florida, the World Conservation Union, Gland, Switzerland and locally the University of the West Indies, Mona, Jamaica and the Ministry of Agriculture. A building has been donated by the government which can be converted to the use of a propagating unit and nursery. The main thrust of this new initiative is the conservation and rescue of native and endemic plants of the island of Jamaica, which are under severe threat from the expanding population and development of the island. In some cases these plants are unique to a particular small area and can be found nowhere else in the island. The second aim of the project is the education of the population about botanical

The bougainvillea walk provides colourful, shady places to sit.

treasures their island possesses. This initiative will include the other botanical gardens of Castleton, Cinchona and Bath – between them they include a wide range of climate and varying ecological conditions. This is an entirely appropriate and suitable use for the gardens and reverts to the original ideals of botanic gardens. It will be a worthwhile, if costly project.

Telephone: 927–7647; (Valerie Stacey) 925–6886

IVOR'S GUEST HOUSE
JACK'S HILL, KINGSTON

There is a long winding road to the very top of Jack's Hill where Ivor's Guest House overlooks Kingston and the valley to the west. Behind it the Blue Mountains rise and there is a view to Newcastle. The Guest House and garden were devastated by Hurricane Gilbert in 1989 but you would never know that now. The main house looks old and traditional but had to be virtually rebuilt. The garden too was blasted, but luckily the two great mango trees (*Mangifera indica*) which frame the view from the veranda survived. One is draped in orchids, the other in philodendron. Pots stand about near the veranda steps filled with balsam, begonias and spider plants.

Narrow terraces and steps drop down the steep hill and, because of the steepness, often one is looking into the tops of trees below and can see hummingbirds working the blossoms. The owners', the Aitkens', only criterion is to plant shrubs and trees that will attract birds. There are a lot of the usual trees seen in tropical gardens – bauhinias, mangoes, oranges, palms and many hibiscus, Mrs Aitken's favourite, in different colours. Crotons and *Plumbago capensis* line the drive and a very old double jasmine scrambles through another mango. On the fence round the kitchen courtyard is a jade vine (*Strongylodon macrobotrys*). Down the hill below one of the cottages in the grounds there are several yellow pouis (*Tabebuia serratifolia*), the red Chinese hat (*Holmskioldia sanguinea*), red ixora (*I. coccinea*), the African tulip tree (*Spathodea campanulata*) and groups of

This view over Kingston is spectacular at any hour.

red and variegated heliconia. Ferns line the terrace walls and behind the house is a bottlebrush tree (*Callistemon lanceolatus*). Along the drive there are a citrus orchard and stands of bougainvillea. Some roses even grow in the cooler air up here, plus great bushes of poinsettia and dracaena. You can stay at the Guest House or just go for a meal or drink. It is very peaceful sitting on the veranda at any time, looking out over Kingston, lit at night by twinkling lights.

Hotel
Telephone (Mrs Aitken): 927–1460

STRAWBERRY HILL
IRISH TOWN, ST ANDREW

Strawberry Hill has been a small hotel for many years but recently it has undergone a great deal of renovation and expansion. The estate was a coffee plantation in the latter part of the eighteenth century. Bath Botanic Garden was also a coffee plantation. The present main house is very like a Swiss mountain chalet, which is appropriate as the site is up a long mountain road towards Newcastle, high above Kingston. The recent renovations have taken the form of building chalets both up and down the mountainside from the main house. These chalets are extremely private, each with their own piece of garden and an amazing view of the plain below and the Blue Mountains behind. Because of the steeply sloping site, the view is often down on to the many pergolas and their creeping, climbing plants, such as red bougainvillea and orange 'bignonia' (*Campsis radicans*). The charm of this garden lies not only because unusual plants are used, but in the way in which they are used so that the colours are good in contrast and co-ordination. Some of this is due to the talent of the Hawaiian gardener who has a very good knowledge of plants. Because the climate of the garden partakes of both the heat of the plain and the coolness of the mountain it is planned to bring sasanqua camellias, Satsuki azaleas and Kurume asiatic rhododendrons to grow here.

Beside the entrance to the main building the planting is in red and yellow. On one side is a *Spathodea campanulata* partly entwined with orange bougainvillea with red

heliconia in front and monstera below. On the other side are the sealing wax palms (*Cyrtostachys renda*), dracaena and more monstera plus a new yellow hybrid of the *Campsis radicans* creeper from South Africa – a pretty plant – and *Solandra guttata* draping the fencing of the path up the hill. There are also ixoras, a plant much used in this garden. All this is backed by great clumps of bamboo. Up the hill, a vast old tree trunk has fallen across the path making an arch and this is host for a large jade vine (*Strongylodon macrobotrys*). At the corner an old root has been used like a piece of sculpture. There is a purple azalea hedge here too which suggests that the plan to import other acid-loving plants is feasible.

As the path climbs to the top lawns there are banks of yellow daylilies (*Hemerocallis*), daylily of a new hybrid. Orange lilies and tree ferns (*Cyathea*) have been planted as sentinels on the bank. A *Solandra guttata* is also here.

At the top of the hill there are more new buildings – the restaurants and bar and a big open courtyard. Old orange tree tubs are to be used here. The lawns are surrounded by curving shrub borders, the lawns themselves concealing water-storage tanks. There are torch lilies (*Etlingera elatior*) in the borders and a tibouchina grown to tree size. Virginia cedars have been used in places and *Congea tomentosa* or the poor man's orchid vine grows here too. The unusual sausage tree (*Kigelia pinnata*) has grown here from seed in ten years. It has grown remarkably well. The trellis is to have another jade vine and other similar creepers. The

A good example of the planting colour schemes at Strawberry Hill.

large *Cedrela odorata*, a Jamaican native, is 110 years old. There is a collection of cycads.

The path leads steeply down the hill again to the newly-built cottages. This steepness has its own problems, one being that drainage is almost too quick. Every inch of soil seems to be covered with plants. Some are trees like the white datura and the bombax, and there are older erythrinas and coffee trees, plus rattan palms or bull thatch the leaves of which are used for roofing. There are also the rose-apple with its white fluffy ball blossoms and white bauhinia – these grow over the lower cottages. Further away on the hillside may be seen teak, jakfruit (*Artocarpus heteropyllus*), the blue mahoe, lignum vitae, soursop (*Annona muricata*) and sweet sop, all remnants of the former plantation. Each cottage seems to have its own colour scheme – blue and white thunbergia covers one, clerodendron and yellow and orange *Campsis radicans* another, pink heliconias (*H. wagneriana*), palms and coralita (*Antigonon leptopus*) another, yellow heliconia (*H. caribaea*) under-planted with yellow *Campsis radicans* yet another. This is a garden worth visiting for the way the plants are used.

Hotel and shop
Telephone (Mr Jonathan Surtees): 944–8400

An old cedar makes a dramatic arch over the path and acts as host to a large jade vine.

MARSHALL'S PEN GREAT HOUSE
MANDEVILLE

This charming old house is one of the fine eighteenth century houses of Jamaica, noted for its garden and bird sanctuary and lived in by the Sutton family. Mr Sutton senior and his wife bought the estate in 1939. He had always loved the house and was delighted when the chance came to acquire it. They then set to and made the garden. Mrs Sutton wrote the first botanical book on the local wildflowers and illustrated it with her own drawings and paintings. Their son Robert, who now farms the estate, wrote *Birds of Jamaica* and is still banding birds for record purposes.

The entrance drive winds across a large park complete with big trees standing on their own, more like England than Jamaica. This is a working farm of approximately 300 acres breeding red poll cattle and selling the stock to local farmers to improve local cattle. It has been a farm for a very long time; the land was bought in 1795 by the Earl of Balcarres who had a house built. It was a coffee plantation at first. There are dry-stone walls dividing the fields. There are very large terraces below the house which are known locally as 'barbecues'. They contain water-storage tanks. The mortar for these walls was mixed with molasses. Large trees dominate the garden. There is a very big bullet wood or balata (*Mimusops globosa*), which has red-coloured wood and from which gutta-percha is obtained, a large poinciana (*Delonix regia*) and two *Cedrela odorata* or West Indian cedar which is used for cabinet making and has a sweet scent.

Mr Sutton's collection of begonias and other pot plants.

There is also a yellow poui (*Tabebuia serratifolia*) and, unusually for Jamaica, there are 24 Bermuda cedars (*Juniperus bermudiana*), big trees now 55 years old. As they are still under threat from a blight in their native island it is good to see them growing here. The 'red earth' soil here is over limestone and contains iron and bauxite (a bauxite factory is not far away). The whole valley appears sheltered but wind can funnel up from the north.

When the Suttons bought the old house, its entrance faced the other way. Originally the ground floor was used for preparing coffee beans and only the first floor was used for living. The Suttons turned it round giving it entrance stairs and the veranda running along the front. This has now been made into a very pleasant feature with a lawn and flower beds in front of the house and its wing. Locally-made pots stand on the steps leading up to the veranda and in the shade below. These pots contain Mr Sutton's collections of begonias from many different countries which he has been collecting for years. He has a white one from Guatemala and a pink and white form from Panama amongst others.

On and under the big trees outside there are orchids growing – a *Vanda suavis* under the poinciana as well as a *V. tricolor*. There is a tiny cattleya-like plant whose flowers last only a day. One of the big trees is a rain tree or guango (*Samanea saman*); near it is a Jamaican brunfelsia, related to *B. americana*, or lady of the night. There is also *Oplonia*

microphylla with its purplish mauve blossoms. Another interesting shrub beside the drive is the endemic *Euphorbia punicea* which has most attractive red blossoms. These shrubs were collected from the Cockpit Country as seedlings. Scattered about on the trees are bromeliads. On the slope beside the house is a shade house for anthuriums and on the house are pyrostegia and staghorn ferns hanging in baskets. The slope up the hill is covered with agapanthus, used as an underplanting for the trees; in front of these are more anthuriums. Finally there is a citrus orchard. A great speciality of Marshall's Pen is the ugli fruit – a cross between grapefruit and mandarin orange. It has been grown on the estate for a long time – this was probably one of the first places in Jamaica to grow it.

This charming garden is open most days but a telephone call is required first in case it is not convenient.

Telephone (Mr Robert Sutton): 963–8569

THREE

THE VIRGIN ISLANDS

Introduction and history

The islands were named by Christopher Columbus. Wishing to call all of the islands which he discovered after saints, the large number of islands and islets in this group suggested to him the idea of calling them after St Ursula and her eleven thousand virgins. Later Columbus recorded that the largest of the islands, St Croix, when he first saw it on his second voyage in 1493, had the appearance of one large, luxurious garden.

Gardening climate

Although tropical in climate, the islands are directly in the path of cooling trade winds which gives them one of the most pleasant year-round climates in the world. There is considerable variation in rainfall between the west and the east side of most islands. On St Croix, for example, the

The beautifully perfumed frangipani is commonly seen.

difference is very marked, the east side being low, arid and rocky, supporting only dry-climate plants, while the western side is higher, wetter, forested and supports wet-tropical climate plants.

Gardening soils

With the exception of Anegada, which is a coral atoll with limestone soils, all of the Virgin islands are of volcanic origin and so have acid soils. However many of the soils today are thin and poor, the result of over-intensive agriculture in the past.

Gardening history

The group of islands today comprises the British Virgin Islands and the US Virgin Islands, the latter having been purchased by the US from Denmark as recently as 1917.

Amerindian settlers were replaced by European settlers in the early seventeenth century but initially only subsistence gardening was carried on. Later, what are now the US Virgin Islands developed sophisticated sugar-based economies. Large plantation houses and their gardens were developed. The best surviving of these is Whim Great

House on St Croix which is surrounded by huge tamarind trees. The tamarind originated in Arabia but was brought to the Caribbean in the early seventeenth century and used widely as a shade tree thereafter. The peak period for population in the Virgin Islands was reached in 1835 after which it declined in parallel with the decline of the sugar trade. In the nineteenth century, however, elegant Government House gardens were made on Tortola and on St Thomas, by the Danish Colonial Council between 1865 and 1887.

Such was the economic decline in the region that, when the 1884 programme to develop botanic gardens and stations throughout the British-owned islands in the Caribbean was developed, the British Virgin Islands were omitted on the grounds they could not afford to support one financially. However, the acute need for an agricultural station to develop new economic crops suited to the Virgin Islands' particular climate and soils was later recognised and an agricultural station was established in 1901. The present botanic garden was laid out on part of its site.

By 1916, the Danes were so concerned about the future economic prospects for their islands that they arranged to sell them to the United States who were anxious to have them for security reasons. They remained under US Navy jurisdiction until 1931.

In the 1950s Laurance S Rockefeller bought large areas of the Virgin Islands subsequently donating the major part of his purchases for the creation of national parks. His donations included about two-thirds of the island of St John (which opened as a US National Park in 1956), the mountain known as Sage Mountain on Tortola and the areas known as Spring Bay and Devil's Bay on Virgin Gorda. The latter areas were given to the British Virgin Islands government which formed the BVI National Parks Trust to look after them. Concurrent with these gifts, Laurance Rockefeller developed two resort areas, Little Dix Bay on St John and Caneel Bay on Virgin Gorda which were designed in a way which was mindful of ecology and protective of the environment, setting a standard for the region that has seldom been equalled since.

For the garden lover, the flowers growing wild in the National Parks are a particular attraction. For example, in the rainforest of Mount Sage National Park on Tortola, many orchids and anthuriums can be seen growing under the tall mahogany cedar and bullet wood trees. In the same location the stunning palicourea – with contrasting black fruit and red flowers on a yellow stalk – thrives. In the low-lying scrub of the coastal areas frangipani can often be seen in flower. On St John, a huge forest of *Pimenta racemosa*, the bay rum tree which produces bay rum oil and hair dressings can be admired. Exotic trees also add their flower colour. The African tulip tree, *Spathodea campanulata*, a native of West Africa, is particularly prominent throughout St Croix whereas the jacaranda, *Jacaranda mimosifolia*, is a native of Brazil which can be enjoyed throughout the islands.

By 1970, over 60 per cent of the population of the US Virgin Islands was employed in tourism, an indication of the importance of the growth of the industry in the second half of the twentieth century. As a means of providing visitor attractions as well as a means of conserving the endemic vegetation of the islands, a series of three botanic gardens have been established and can be visited – on Tortola, on St Thomas and on St Croix. Gardening today is not without its problems. Wild donkeys, if unchecked, could destroy gardens on St John. Huge iguanas eat hibiscus flowers on St Croix. Although the history of gardening in the Virgin Islands is a modest one when compared with that of other islands in the Caribbean, it nonetheless represents a significant part of their history and present environment.

Now grown all over the tropics, the jacaranda's blue blossoms are a beautiful sight.

Gardens

ESTATE ST PETER GREATHOUSE
ST THOMAS

Although St Thomas is among the more developed of the Caribbean islands, it retains much woodland throughout its countryside and a historic quarter of great importance in its capital, Charlotte Amalie (named after a Danish queen). In the latter, the garden enthusiast can wander with profit through the flower-filled lanes and up steep flights of stone steps to admire the Danish colonial houses behind hedges of bougainvillea and oleander, and under the shade of flamboyant and jacaranda trees.

Few of the great plantation houses of St Thomas survive. Fewer still are complimented by gardens. Estate St Peter Greathouse is therefore an important part of the island's heritage. It is reached along the St Peter Mountain Road, a continuation of the scenic mountain road known as Skyline Drive, from which both sides of the island, that facing the Atlantic Ocean and that facing the Caribbean Sea, can be seen simultaneously. The second highest peak along this ridge of mountains is St Peter Mountain at 1500 feet. The volcanic soils, higher rainfall and cooling trade winds make this quieter, northern region of the island better gardening country than the drier, more populated areas of the south.

Estate St Peter Greathouse and its eleven acres were bought in 1987 by Mr and Mrs Howard Lawson de Wolfe. They began the restoration of the house and garden, and the creation of a new botanic garden. Their new tropical paradise was badly damaged two years later in Hurricane Hugo but sufficiently recovered to open to the public again in 1992. Today there are over 500 plant species growing in a dramatically landscaped setting of waterfalls and reflecting pools high above which are decks with stunning views over the island's irregular coastline with its horseshoe shaped beaches and wooded promontories. Among the interesting native trees to be observed in the woods are the highly-ornamental lignum vitae (*Guaiacum officinale*), whose dense hard wood was once used to carve idols and which continues to hold a place both in Caribbean folklore and herbal medicine. Part of the garden is developed as an orchid jungle in which both native and exotic orchids are grown in an apparently natural way on trees. The tree species used in establishing such an area should not only provide the necessary overhead shade but also their bark should be capable of promoting root attachment. Native trees such as lignum vitae (*Guaiacum officinale*), frangipani (*Plumeria alba*) and calabash (*Crescentia cujete*) as well as naturalised trees such as flamboyant (*Delonix regia*) and mango (*Mangifera indica*) are among the best for this purpose.

Another area is conserved as rainforest – an especially important venture when much of the Caribbean's rainforest has already gone. This area of the garden is of particular interest on account of the way in which it addresses one of the great questions of contemporary gardening: the relationship between gardening and conservation. Nearby, a small area has been reserved as a monkey habitat.

The calabash tree (*Crescentia cujete*). (Chris Huxley)

Gardens open to the public but created through private initiative are few in the Caribbean which is why the Estate St Peter Greathouse gardens could become a model for similar enterprises on other islands in the future.

Gardens open daily 9.00 am – 4.30 pm.
Telephone: 809–774–4999
Fax: 809–774–1723

Joseph Reynold O'Neal
Botanic Gardens,
ROAD TOWN, TORTOLA

The Joseph Reynold O'Neal Botanic Gardens are located on the north-western outskirts of Road Town, Tortola's capital, on a site which was once part of the experimental agricultural and horticultural station established in 1900. The purpose of the station was to undertake trials of crops such as coffee, cacao and limes which might replace the sugar crop on the island, which was then suffering an economic decline. Directors of the garden were appointed from the Royal Botanic Gardens at Kew one of whom, Mr Fishlock, reported in 1904 that one of the handicaps to progress in the garden was that neither spades nor forks could be used in cultivation as most people who were employed at the station, being unshod, could only work with a hoe. However, in the long term, lack of investment in the establishment of new crops meant the usefulness of the experimental station was limited and it was gradually run down until the remaining four acres were taken over for the creation of the present Botanic Gardens in 1986.

The driving force behind the new garden's creation was Joseph Reynold O'Neal, after whom the garden is now named, but many other local residents volunteered help and continue to do so. Donations were sought through the British Virgin Islands National Parks Trust. (The trust now

The central focus of the garden, the three-tier, cast-iron fountain.
(Helen Gasneal)

The tool shed in the Joseph Reynold O'Neal Garden. (Helen Gasneal)

has no fewer than eleven areas under its management and has inaugurated a 'plant-a-tree' campaign which is designed to allow every resident and visitor to the island a chance to contribute to the re-afforestation of the land acquired by the trust.) Local residents and commercial enterprises, visitors as well as those who have vacation homes on the island, either contributed to the garden's general development fund or else gave money for specific areas or features planned for the garden.

The confined, four-acre site is surrounded by a screen of trees and divided by an avenue of Puerto Rican royal palms (*Roystonea borinquena*) which leads from the entrance gate to a grand, three-tiered Victorian-style cast-iron fountain which forms the central focus of the garden. Under the palm avenue have been planted borders planned to feature flowers and foliage plants in the hotter colours – reds, yellows, oranges and dusky pinks. Chief among these are the sturdy, evergreen ixoras but there are also chenille plants (*Acalypha hispida*) with their long, purple-red tassels, shrimp plants in variety and a clump of red fountain grass (*Pennisetum setaceum*, 'Rubrum'). Around the fountain cluster a set of four classic wooden garden benches set against sheltering hedges of the aromatic orange jasmine (*Murraya paniculata*). The garden is bisected in the other direction by a long pergola walk. On its stout, wooden structure are grown many of the most vigorous woody climbers associated with tropical gardens. A balanced choice has been made – bougainvilleas to flower during the dry season, the purple wreath (*Petrea volubilis*) to show its colour after rain, the blue and the white trumpet vines which open a daily supply of new flowers over a long season. The path underneath is edged with ribbons of Madagascar periwinkle (*Catharanthus roseus*), which is quite happy in a dry location in the garden.

The palm avenue and the pergola walk divide, between them, the garden into four quarters, each of which has been developed with its own distinct design and planting theme. The Christmas garden is centred on a large curving lawn like a green lake with planted bays and promontories. The planted areas contain a mixture of shrubs, subshrubs, perennials and annuals which are grouped and graded according to colour and height in the same way that an English-style mixed border is, except that, of course, in this case the plants themselves are tropical species. A Norfolk Island pine (*Araucaria heterophylla*), a fulcrum plant in the garden, has leaned precariously since the time of Hurricane Hugo yet continues to flourish.

The palm grove is an eye-opener for those who think of the palm family as containing nothing but a dull range of plants depressingly similar in colour and form. Here the trunk of the sealing wax palm (*Cyrtostachys renda*), in which bright red and green portions alternate, alerts the visitor to the wide variety of trunk form within the family. The foliage of the round leaf palm (*Licuala grandis*) illustrates just one of the family's many different leaf forms. The grey leaf and white petiole of the latania fan palm (*Latania loddigesii*) illustrate the palm family's range of foliage colour. The bright red, egg-shaped fruits of *Veitchia merrillii* show how decorative a palm's fruit can be. Also

The cereus blooms at night but the blossoms last on a wet morning.

featured in the palm grove, and of particular interest to those interested in natural vegetation, are palms which are native to the Caribbean area itself. Of pre-eminent interest is the tall, slender broom palm (*Coccothrinax alta*), the only palm which is native to the Virgin Islands. Also represented are several *Pandanus* and *Cycas* species which, despite their appearance, are neither palm nor fern.

Fascinating for the owner of a dry, seaside garden is the area known as the cactus and succulent garden. Here groups of agaves, aloes and yuccas combine with the flat hand cactus (*Opuntia* spp.) and columnar cactus (*Cereus* spp.) (many of the latter being Caribbean natives) to form a garden of rich formal contrasts. The collection is extended by growing some plants which cannot be included in the cactus or succulent plant families but which nevertheless

The ornamental *Miconia magnifica*, a native of Jamaica.

are sufficiently robust to withstand exposed or seaside locations. These include the pitch apple or autograph tree (*Clusia rosea*) with tough, leathery leaves strong enough to scratch messages on and the felt plant (*Calotropis procera*), with coarse woolly leaves.

A perimeter path winds around the edge of the garden passing, in succession, a fern house of airy lattice-work, an enclosed orchid house and a delightful tool shed constructed in a West Indian local style and painted sky-blue. It also passes through densely-planted areas in which are grown trees and shrubs which do not fit into the main themed areas of the garden but which are nevertheless judged to be a vital part of the garden's collection. At one point along the perimeter path is a small lake which has been developed with water-lilies, water hyacinths and papyrus as a water garden. Across a bridge is the rainforest garden – a simulation of indigenous rainforest where plant collections are allowed to run riot. Anthuriums and red gingers grow in abandon and are interspersed with ferns and twining philodendrons. One patch has been taken over by heliconias. A tall sandbox tree (*Hura crepitans*) supplies the necessary shade.

Although the prime instigator of the garden was Joseph Reynold O'Neal, the main designer was Margaret Barwick, wife of the then Governor of the British Virgin Islands. She laid out the garden in 1985 and it was first opened to the public in 1986. Just as the garden was becoming more established, Hurricane Hugo struck in September 1989. Most of the big trees were destroyed. Many of the remaining plants still bear the scars of its devastation. However, the garden was replenished by gifts of plants from supporters and it now has a propagation house of its own. The soil is naturally rocky so much topsoil was, and continues to be, brought in. A 60-feet deep well supplies water for an automatic irrigation system. Even so, many plants, and especially rainforest plants, suffer acutely in the dry season. However, the garden remains one of the principal oases of good garden design and horticulture in the Caribbean.

Gardens open daily 8.00 am – 5.30 pm.
Telephone: 494–4557

St George's Botanical Garden
ST CROIX

Centreline Road, the road between St Croix's two principal towns, Christiansted and Frederiksted, is also known as Queen Mary's Highway after a Danish queen. The parallel road to the north traverses what remains of St Croix's rainforest and is lined with the dark glossy foliage of huge mahogany trees, so the road is known as Mahogany Road. Lying between the two is St George's Botanical Garden. The site is that of an eighteenth and nineteenth century Danish sugar estate and the 16-acre garden is laid out around the workers' village. An archaeological dig in 1976 uncovered beneath the ruins what would seem to be the largest of the 96 known Arawak settlements on St Croix dating from AD 100–900.

The garden, which began as a clean-up project of the local garden club in 1972, is privately-funded and volunteer-managed. Some buildings have been restored but others, conserved as ruins, are used as backgrounds for landscaped plantings. The overall garden design, however, combines areas of natural vegetation with areas of landscaped plantings and open space. Approximately 500 tree and plant species found on site are being conserved as part of the garden club's ambition to assist in the conservation of the native St Croix flora. This project will also involve growing samples of all of St Croix's endangered endemic species: the present collection includes two: the St Croix agave and a touch-me-not. Of course it is preferable that such rare endemics should be conserved *in situ* in the wild through the creation of protected reserves. However, with increasing pressure on rare plant habitats, it is also provident to undertake a programme of *ex situ* conservation, for example, in botanic gardens, as well.

Another important project being undertaken by St George's Botanical Garden is an historical one – to make a collection of the five dozen or so plants that the Spanish botanist, Gonzalo Fernandez de Oviedo, listed in his *Summary of the Natural and General History of the West Indies*, a report on New World flora presented to Queen Isabella in 1526. The Spaniards, being the first Europeans to explore the Caribbean, were the first Europeans to describe botanically the native plants of the region, particularly of Hispaniola and Cuba, the islands which saw their first major settlements.

In about 1550, during the reign of Philip II, Nicholas Morandes, a Sevillean doctor wrote his *Medicinal History of the Items Brought from the West Indies*. These were but partial treatments however. In 1570, Philip II commissioned a comprehensive study of the *natural, ancient and political history of New Spain* from one of his palace physicians, Francisco Hernandez (1514–87). Its sixteen volumes – the result of seven years of fieldwork – were deposited in the library of the royal palace of Escorial but were never published. P M Anglerius in his book *The History of Travels in the West and East Indies* (1577) described the Spaniards' interest in the *the uses to which the natives put the plants; their use in the fabrication of household utensils and in the making of herbal medicines and poisons*. The project of the St George's Botanical Garden which aims to recreate this historical collection of plants will help visitors to the garden to

The double red hibiscus

A large frangipani tree

understand in a vivid way the early history of botany in the Caribbean.

The St George's Botanical Garden has many horticultural and botanical displays to attract the casual visitor. The entrance drive is bordered by royal palms and bougainvillea leading to towering kapok and tamarind trees, multi-coloured hibiscus and many-coloured frangipani and a vast poinsettia bed, almost a quarter of an acre of red and white blooms from December to March. There are over 350 introduced or exotic tree and plant species, including two outstanding specimens of the sago palm, not palms as the name would imply but relations of the cycads and so survivors from a pre-Ice Age vegetation.

The conversion of some of the former sugar estate buildings into a library, a plant nursery and a gift shop ensure the garden attracts a wide range of interested people from the casual visitor to the serious botanist.

Gardens open Monday through Friday 9.00 am to 3.00 pm.
Telephone: 692–2874
Fax: 692–2874

Gazetteer of other gardens in the Virgin Islands

⚘ CANEEL BAY RESORT ⚘
ST JOHN, USVI

Built in 1952 by Laurance S Rockefeller on the 170-acre site of a mid-eighteenth century sugar plantation, the resort structures are built in wood and stone and are surrounded by a range of skilfully-planted gardens which feature trees such as the flamboyant (*Delonix regia*), the golden shower (*Cassia fistula*) the geranium tree (*Cordia sebestena*) and the native sea-grape (*Coccoloba uvifera*) and shrubs such as ixoras, bougainvilleas, oleanders, hibiscus and poinsettias.

Open to hotel guests only, or occasional horticultural groups by appointment.

⚘ GOVERNMENT HOUSE GARDENS ⚘
CHARLOTTE AMALIE, ST THOMAS USVI

Built for the Danish Government of St Thomas in 1865–7, Government House has a small but historically interesting terraced garden centred on a two-tiered antique fountain. The garden acts as a formal foreground to the extensive view over Charlotte Amalie Harbour, its wooded islands and the distant sea.

Cassia fistula, better known as golden shower, is one of the most spectacular of trees.

❧LAVALETTE HOUSE HOTEL,❧
(1829 HOTEL)
CHARLOTTE AMALIE, ST THOMAS, USVI

An old urban mansion house dating from 1829 with a courtyard swathed in bougainvillea and filled with the sound of splashing water which, with its historic atmosphere, make it one of the most romantic town gardens in the Caribbean.

Open to hotel guests only.

❧FIRST LADY'S GARDEN❧
ROAD TOWN, TORTOLA, BVI

Located on a hill to the south-west of Road Town, the gardens of the imposing, white-painted mansion have been revitalised in recent years, principally by Mrs Margaret Barwick, wife of a recent Governor.

Open occasionally by appointment only.
Telephone: 774–0001 x 4310
Fax: 774–1361

❧LITTLE DIX BAY RESORT❧
VIRGIN GORDA, BVI

Built in 1964 on a 500-acre private reserve around a crescent-shaped bay, it is a sister resort to Caneel Bay on St John and was also developed by Laurance S Rockefeller in a way that is mindful of ecology and protective of the natural environment. Located above it is the Gorda Peak National Park with an abundance of trails and many orchids blooming, particularly after the December rains.

Open to hotel guests only or occasional horticultural groups by appointment.

FOUR

THE LEEWARD ISLANDS

Introduction and history

In the days of sail, the orientation of a country or an island to the prevailing wind was an important factor in its overall economy and development. For example, the southern coast of Portugal is still divided into those areas which are *barlavento*, windward and those areas which are *sotovento*, leeward. So it was when some of the islands of the Caribbean came to be grouped by name. The group of islands of the Lesser Antilles which was aligned or oriented away from the prevailing wind was named The Leeward Islands. This is not to imply that they are not subject to wind – indeed refreshing wind is one of their main attractions – but that as a group they are not aligned head-on to them. The Leeward Islands include Anguilla, Antigua and Barbuda, St Kitts and Nevis, and Montserrat.

This view of Admiral's Inn shows only part of the successful restoration of Nelson's dockyard.

Gardening climate

Although the average temperatures in the Leeward Islands are approximately the same as in the Virgin Islands, the range of temperatures is greater – some degrees hotter in summer and cooler in winter. The rainy season lasts from May/June to November/December except on the drier islands of Anguilla and Antigua where it is considerably shorter, lasting only from September to December and where a different range of plant material has therefore to be used. A critical factor in the selection of plants for a garden depends on the garden's height above sea-level. For example, H N Coleridge in his book *Six Months in the West Indies* (1826) notes with amazement that as many of the plantation houses on St Kitts were located high up on the mountain slopes, the temperatures were low enough to grow European vegetables such as sea-kale, turnips and carrots and European fruits such as peaches and strawberries.

Gardening soils

The Leeward Islands embrace a mixture of soils. Anguilla and Barbuda being coral have dry, limestone soils covered with scrub which looks like a brown African savanna during the dry season of the year. However, St Kitts, Nevis and Montserrat are of volcanic origin and have fertile, lava-type soils. Antigua has a mixture of both, the most fertile soils in the south-west of the island and on which the delicious black Antigua pineapple is grown are volcanic in origin. Soils vary greatly in fertility even within an individual island. Although the soils of the Lesser Antilles are not, in general, so fertile as those of the Greater Antilles such as Cuba or Hispaniola, the soils in St Kitts are such that in the eighteenth century they produced the highest-yielding sugar-cane crop in the world. The part of St Kitts which is to the east of the mountains is more fertile than that to the west due to a greater deposit of volcanic material on that side. Around the small village of Gingerland on the east side, the soil's exceptional fertility results in high-yielding crops of ginger root, cinnamon and nutmeg but all round St Kitts the rich abundance of flowers and fruit evident in the roadside gardens testifies to its rich soils.

Gardening history

There are extensive remains on Anguilla and Antigua of Amerindian agriculture. On Anguilla the ubiquitous limestone cave system provided fresh water reservoirs as well as shelter for the inhabitants of the island as early as the fifth century AD. These early peoples carried on subsistence gardening, producing crops such as cassava which, when they had successfully learned to leach it of its poisonous juice, became the staple food and was deified as the god Yocahu.

With the exception of Anguilla, which was not colonised until 1650, the Leeward Islands were occupied by European settlers in the early half of the seventeenth century. There was an early interest in the botany of native plants, particularly with regard to their medical uses. A surgeon called G Horsnell (1625–97) who corresponded with John Ray, the London scientist who also studied plants, was among the first but there were many others.

St Kitts was settled by Captain Warner in 1623 as part of a pattern of new settlement. When the settlers had landed and erected minimal shelter for themselves, they immediately planted a garden, using seeds they had brought with them to grow provisions for the future. Captain Warner also planted tobacco, through the sale of which he hoped to raise capital to improve the new colony. However, the fledgling trade soon foundered on account of the superiority of Virginia tobacco and the inhabitants of St Kitts switched to growing sugar. By the mid-seventeenth century the economic importance of sugar had been discovered and gradually islands like Antigua, St Kitts and Nevis were turned over to a virtual monoculture of that crop. Wisely, the high mountain areas on St Kitts were reserved as rainforest to attract cloud and rain which after falling in the mountains would flow down the island's narrow ravines by swift streams from which it could be distributed to the cultivated land below, providing the best possible supply of fresh water in the these areas. With the water came a rich volcanic silt to nourish the soils.

The planter families over a period of time came to enjoy an elegant way of life. In 1826, H N Coleridge was delighted by the plantation houses and gardens on Antigua:

Stately mansions with English parks and lawns about them, and occupied by the hereditary planter families – Cedar Hill, approached through a long avenue of white cedar trees; Betty's Hope with its pillared gateway; the impressive estate of Green Castle.

The flower gardens of the plantation houses he found particularly enchanting with *scarlet cordias, and the saffron and crimson fences of hibiscus, and the massy radiance of tropical leaves.* Janet Schaw had previously (1774–6) been struck by the way in which the Antiguan planters had used shade trees to protect their houses from the sun. Of Skerrets Plantation (later to become the site of Antigua's botanic garden) she wrote that it was *laid out with groves, gardens and delightful walks of Tamarind trees, which give the finest shade you can imagine,* and went on to describe, on another plantation: *the Palmetto tree, with which this lady's house is surrounded and entirely guarded by them from the intense heat. They are in general from forty to sixty feet high before they put out a branch, and as straight as a line.*

Of the effects of the 1772 hurricane on the palmettos on another plantation, Eleonora, she wrote: *the Palmettos stand shattered monuments of that fatal calamity; with these the house was surrounded in the same manner, as I described the plantation near the town ... his orange orchyards, Tammerand walks and Cocoa trees torn from the roots ....* Lines of planted palm trees also characterised the St Kitts landscape. Charles

The white cedar is seen in almost all the islands.

Kingsley in 1871 was ambivalent about their effect in the landscape:

Tall Cabbage palms ... Palmistes as the French call them, seem incongruous away from their native forests, as they have been here planted along roadsides and around fields, or near engine works or towering above the rich shrubberies which shrouded comfortable country houses.

A colourful bromeliad. (Chris Huxley)

As on other groups of islands, medical doctors were to the fore in botanising, collecting plants which might be of medical use and sending them for examination and cultivation in London. For example, John Ryan MD collected plants on Montserrat, sending seed to the Chelsea Physic Garden in London in 1778.

As in other areas of the Caribbean, the depressed sugar economy led to the search for viable alternative crops. The Leeward Islands took part in the establishment of the great federation of botanic gardens and stations set up throughout the Caribbean at the end of the nineteenth century, individual gardens being created on Antigua, Montserrat and St Kitts.

The botanic station on Antigua was established in 1889 on the former Skerrets estate near the capital, St Johns. It was in a dry, windy location and its soil was a heavy clay on which great quantities of drought-loving plants, particularly economic plants like hemp and sisal, were established. Because of the wide variety of Antigua's soils, two outlying botanic stations were set up, one at Body Ponds to the north-east of the volcanic section of the island in a sheltered valley that might be suitable for growing nutmeg and cacao and the other at Copse Cross in the southern part of the island near English Harbour, where the black pineapple is grown. However, in 1897, all of the garden's activity was suddenly stopped by the refusal of some members of the island's Legislative Council to pass the curator's salary on the grounds the colony could not afford it. After this the garden and its stations carried on, but in a crippled condition.

On Montserrat, a botanic station was established in 1890 on a quarter-acre site by the sea on which the curator grew a great variety of vegetables on an experimental basis. It was shut down in 1897 on account of the island's straitened circumstances. A second and more successful attempt to start a garden was made in 1901. Three agricultural stations were set up, at Grove Estate, Harris' Village and Olveston respectively under the direction of Mr J A Jordan. Grove Estate near Plymouth was to combine the function of botanic garden with that of an agricultural station. The garden survives today but in a much reduced state as a result of the devastation caused by Hurricane Hugo in 1989.

Young curators like Mr Jordan, who was born in Northumberland, England, were selected for service in the tropics by the Royal Botanic Gardens, Kew usually after

The bees are attracted to the petrea plant.

the young employee had served his apprenticeship in the hothouses there, where he would have gained some experience of tropical plants. Subsequently, they kept in touch with their colleagues throughout the tropical world through the *Journal of the Kew Guild*, the organisation of past students of Kew. For example, Mr Jordan wrote in the journal in 1904:

The work is getting on very well here at Montserrat, both in the garden and among the people. One of our objects is to train boys at the station and in this I have been very successful. I have now more applications than I can entertain and am able to select the more promising boys. The earlier started among them are now loaned out to planters to spray, prune, bind, etc. and are in constant demand… The spring flowers if they may be so called are

heralding the approach of the rainy season and the wastelands are bright with Hippeastrum equense. *The rocky sides of the ravines are pretty with the long racemes of the metallic-blue flowered* Petraea volubilis, *Mango, Hog plums, Red and White Cedars and many other trees are now making the place gay with their blossoms.*

Jordan's career, like that of many of his colleagues, was cut short by tropical fever and disease. Mr J H Hart, Superintendent of the Botanic and Agricultural Department, Trinidad, wrote to the Director of Kew in 1906:

A.J. Jordan died after a short illness of some six days of pernicious remittant fever … Mr. Jordan was a man of sincere religious convictions. He married after he reached the West Indies and has left a widow and one child. With exemplary forethought, he has made provision for them by adequately insuring his life.

He was 32.

A similar sad fate befell Mr Lunt, curator of the botanic station on St Kitts in 1904. The station had been established in 1891 on part of an old sugar estate, La Guerite, according to a plan laid down by Daniel Morris, then Assistant Director of the Royal Botanic Gardens, Kew. In 1898, William Lunt was appointed curator. He had left Welbeck Abbey Gardens, Nottinghamshire, to study at Kew Gardens in 1892. His taste for, and knowledge of, botany was such that in 1893 he was selected to accompany Theodore Bent on a botanical exploration of the Hadhramaut in Arabia. There he personally discovered two new botanical genera and 25 new species, among the latter *Verbascum luntii* and *Aloe luntii*, which were subsequently called after him. He was then appointed Assistant Superintendent, Trinidad Botanic Gardens from which after four years he went as curator to the botanic station on St Kitts. However, after five years there he fell ill after celebrating New Year's Eve at a friend's house and died three days later on January 3, 1904. His obituary in the *Kew Bulletin* recalls how, in addition to his botanical achievements, he had made the first collection of land-shells in Trinidad when he was stationed on that island and that he was a *lieutenant of Volunteers and a good shot.*

Of private gardens in the Leeward Islands during that period, Daniel Morris, while on his botanical mission to the West Indies in 1891, noticed some interesting examples on Antigua:

At Parham were two interesting private gardens belonging to Mr Freeland and his son, Dr F.J. Freeland, the former has numerous ornamental plants e.g. Crotons, Araucarias, Roses, Orchids and Aroids while the son devotes his leisure time to the cultivation of ferns and palms in pots in a lath-house of pitch-pine covered with creepers.

Of the gardeners in the vicinity of St Johns, the capital of Antigua, he mentions:

Mr Alleyne Archer, a planter who is an enthusiastic horticultur-alist, with a very interesting collection of fruit trees and orna-mental plants; fine plants of Ipomea Horsfalliae, *a large-flowered form of* Antigonon leptopus, *numerous plants in pots of the graceful* Thrinax radiata *which is said to form large thickets on the neighbouring island of Barbuda and a very interesting series*

It may seem surprising to see roses in the Caribbean, but some old-fashioned ones flourish.

of Hibiscus hybrids. *Dr Edwards had a fine plant in flower of* Nomara volubilis *known locally as the 'white convallia', a good plant of* Calliandra purpurea, *originally from Kew and a grape vine, Muscat of Alexandria. Bishop Branch showed me his garden including* Gloriosa superba *and a fine form of* Bougainvillea glabra.

No botanic garden was established on Anguilla but Daniel Morris did visit and there found a palm which was new to science and which was named *Thrinax morrisii* after him.

The twentieth century has seen the growth of tourism in the Leeward Islands as elsewhere in the Caribbean. The 1950s and 1960s saw the beginning of the vogue of converting old plantation houses into elegant hotels. On

Nevis, the house at Rawlins Plantation has become the focus of a small hotel – the windmill has been converted into a guest suite, the boiling houses into a pleasant court-yard for dining. Also on Nevis, the sugar mill of Montpelier Plantation has been converted into an atmospheric hotel. As at Rawlins, the linking element which draws all of the plantation buildings into one landscaped whole is the garden. A successful conversion of a different complex of buildings is that of English Harbour, the eighteenth-century navy yard on Antigua. Here also the landscaped gardens form the link between a diverse group of buildings. On Nevis the birthplace of Alexander Hamilton, the first US Secretary of the Treasury, has been converted into a museum around which has been planted a garden with an extensive representative collection of the native plants of Nevis.

In the wild, there are many flowering plants to excite the interest of the garden lover. For example, the lotus *Nelumbium speciosum* grows in great profusion and flowers during the rainy season in the river beds of Antigua. Passion flowers romp through the roadside hedges on Nevis and, in normal times, a pink-flowered impatiens grows in the forest shade of Galway's Soufriere on Montserrat.

Although less subject to volcanic activity than the Windward Islands further south, the Leeward Islands are more subject to drought and devastating wind. In 1989, many gardens and plants were levelled by Hurricane Hugo. However, the wide variety of the islands' climate and soils make them a source of many different pleasures for the garden visitor.

Gardens

MONTPELIER PLANTATION INN
NEVIS

Montpelier Plantation is located at about 700 feet above sea-level on the southern slope of Mount Nevis. With views to the 3232 feet high volcanic peak behind and to the sea in front, it enjoys a cool, comfortable location for gardening. It also enjoys good soils being located near Gingerland – so called because its rich soils make it the centre of the island's ginger root as well as cinnamon and nutmeg production.

The plantation is well-known as the site of Lord Nelson's marriage to the widowed Frances Herbert Nisbet on March 11th, 1787. Montpelier Great House belonged to Mrs Nisbet's uncle, Mr Herbert, the President of Nevis. Prince William Henry, later Duke of Clarence and King William IV, who was then serving with Nelson's fleet in the Caribbean, gave the bride away. The marriage was registered at nearby St John's Church, Fig Tree Village. Only the gateposts and a few columns of the mansion remain. The island's slow economic decline after the collapse of the sugar industry, together with earthquakes and hurricanes, has meant few of the eighteenth-century plantation houses have survived.

James Milnes Gaskill came to Nevis from Yorkshire in 1963 and bought the plantation. Of the original buildings only the sugar boiling-house and mill had survived. (Because cane-grinding survived in a small way until

World War II, sugar mills often survived the plantation houses to which they were formerly attached.) He set about building the present hotel comprising a central building in traditional Nevisean style and 16 modern but comfortable cottages, each with its own terrace, which were completed in 1967. All of the buildings are constructed with locally-quarried volcanic stone but the central building is surrounded on the first floor by a typical West Indian fretted veranda swathed in bougainvillea.

Today, the visitor turns down a side road through coconut and mango groves and finally arrives through a cloud of bougainvillea at the inn. Bougainvillea is one of the keynote plants of the garden. A classic garden plant all over the tropical world, there are several hundred varieties, some of which like *Bougainvillea* 'Mrs Helen McLean' originated in the Caribbean. It first occurred as a natural mutation in the garden of Mrs McLean of San Fernando, Trinidad. With the inestimable advantage of flowering during the dry season, they can clamber or sprawl in a versatile way over a fence, across a wall or up a tree trunk yet they can also be trained or pruned as required.

The magnificent and extensive gardens at Montpelier Plantation focus on the eighteenth-century sugar mill and a mammoth swimming pool with broad reaches of stone terracing which matches the volcanic stone of the houses. Gently-stepped paving levels in a variety of shapes give a

Flower of the forest, poinciana or royal poinciana (*Delonix regia*). The common names are flamboyant or flame tree. (Chris Huxley)

73

A saman tree (*Samanea saman*) at Romney Manor, St Kitts. (Chris Huxley)

basic geometric structure to the garden which is then softened by the abundant planting in raised beds. Large terracotta pots and natural boulders chosen for their interesting shape and colour are positioned around the terraces to further break up the geometry of the design. Old sugar pans have been pressed into service as garden ponds in which enormous toads live among the water-lilies. The tropical character is enhanced by a host of resident birds such as banana quits, hummingbirds, ground-doves, Caribbean elaenias, black-faced grass quits and the Lesser Antillean bullfinch.

Another keynote plant in the garden is the bearded fig tree, *Ficus citrifolia*, of which there are large specimens with picturesque twisting trunks and aerial roots cascading earthwards from overhanging branches. It is a native of Barbados where unfortunately the original forests have disappeared, only a few isolated specimens remaining, as in Andromeda Gardens and Welchman Hall Gully. Its attractive foliage and spreading habit make it an ideal specimen tree to plant in a large garden.

Traditionally, the Gingerland area of Nevis is the home of good gardens. During the 1970s, for example, it was the location of the most sophisticated private garden on Nevis which belonged to a New England rheumatologist, Dr Scull, with dozens of orchids, bromeliads and other tropical species not normally found on Nevis, as well as a rare collection of citrus trees. Now the area has another important garden. With the hotel having been completely restored and redecorated and the gardens renewed since 1986, it is a rich source of inspiration for the gardening visitor.

Another part of the restored dockyard, English Harbour.

❧ English Harbour ❧
ANTIGUA

Antigua's fine, natural harbours were of crucial importance for the operation of the British fleet in the Caribbean during the seventeenth and eighteenth centuries. The most famous of these was English Harbour which was used as a refuge as early as 1671 and which was established as a naval base between 1725 and 1746. There British ships could be repaired and refitted safe from hurricanes and enemy attack. It was the principal operational base of a succession of renowned admirals including Rodney, Nelson and Cochrane. Its complex of repair yards, workshops, stores, offices, lodgings and admiral's quarters was developed during the long period of its use between 1707 and 1899, by which time most ships had become too large to negotiate the winding harbour entrance. Its heyday was during 1786 when the young Duke of Clarence (later William IV) lived in the harbour when he was in command of the HMS *Pegasus*, a ship in Admiral Lord Nelson's fleet. Nelson was commander of the British navy in the Leeward Islands between 1784 and 1787.

In 1906, the harbour was finally abandoned and subsequently suffered serious earthquake damage. In his book *The Traveller's Tree* (1950), Patrick Leigh Fermor describes his visit to the decaying remains of the Admiral's quarters:

The sad and echoing chambers were decayed almost to the verge of disintegration. We tiptoed from room to room. One hard stomp, you felt, would bring the building down in a heap. The bedrooms, the dining room, the office – these had been the daily background of Nelson for the years which, as captain of HMS Boreas, he had spent on the West Indian station. A figurehead and a little cannon guarded the door, and all over the flat promontory that jutted into English harbour stood the crumbling impedimenta of an eighteenth century naval base.

The only building still in good repair was Clarence House, built on a hill overlooking the harbour for the accommodation of the Duke of Clarence in 1786. It had continued in use, but as the country residence of the Governor-General of the Leeward Islands. It was Earl Baldwin, when Governor-General, who had the initial idea to restore the harbour as a modern yachting and yacht-chartering centre. Sir Kenneth Blackburne, his successor, formed the Society of Friends of English Harbour which raised funds and oversaw the restoration of the complex which since 1985 has been designated a National Park area.

The old boat- and mast-yard were developed as part of the new marina. The wooden, veranda'd structure of the Admiral's House (1855) has been restored as a museum displaying a collection of marine, naval and Nelson memorabilia. The old lead, turpentine and pitch store (planned in 1785 but not completed until 1788) has been converted into an atmospheric inn. Constructed of brick brought from England as ship's ballast and lighted by traditional sash windows, it has the character of a small English manor house. The old copper and lumber store, also built to house materials used in the repair of sailing ships, is also constructed of similar brick and is likewise today an inn of atmospheric character.

Admiral's Inn, now a very comfortable hotel.

Our concern in this book, however, is to introduce the reader to the way in which the whole area of the harbour has been seen and recreated as one integrated landscape or garden setting. First, the harbour as a whole has been viewed as worthy of conservation, the views being enhanced by the picturesque ruins of two forts: Fort Berkeley at the harbour mouth and Shirley Heights (completed in 1787 and named after General Shirley, then Governor of the Leeward Islands) which overlooks the harbour from a hill to the east. Shirley Heights can be reached from the harbour along a footpath which has been laid out as a nature trail – a pamphlet is available describing the trees and other plants encountered along the way together with their medicinal and other practical uses. Clarence House, now open to the public when the

Governor is not in residence, is surrounded by, what one might take at first glance to be, a stretch of English parkland. On closer inspection, however, the scattered groups of trees standing on the rolling greensward turn out to be mahogany trees rather than English beech trees. Nonetheless, they are disposed around the winding carriage drive which leads down from the gates on the high road, and around the mansion house, in the naturally-placed groups that are characteristic of the English landscape style. Nineteenth-century prints of Antiguan plantation houses show them to have been surrounded by small parks in the English style of which the park around Clarence House is a rare and well-preserved example. Along the verandas of the house have been set out garden seats in the Chinese Chippendale style.

The landscaping of the harbour area was conceived by the Friends of English Harbour as an integral part of the whole development. The ancient structures – the piers, jetties, capstans, cast-iron bollards, freestanding boathouse pillars – were retained as sculptural focal elements among the new plantings. The choice of plantings was severely restricted because of the seaside, south-facing location to those which would be both salt- and drought-tolerant. Caribbean royal palms (*Roystonea oleracea*), the native sea grape (*Coccoloba uvifera*), and the Australian casuarina (*Casuarina equisetifolia*), were the trees chosen for the basic background planting. The palms, leaning picturesquely to leeward throughout the area, are the most successful from an aesthetic point of view. The choice of smaller plants was equally restricted. Much use is made, for example, of the Turk's cap cactus (*Melocactus intortus*). This is a native of coastal areas throughout the eastern Caribbean and so well suited to this location. *Yucca* and *Agave* spp., both Central American natives, also adapt well. The latter had been grown since 1896 at the botanical station of Cobb's Cross located above English Harbour and so were well tested in the locality. (The station was a subsidiary of the principal botanic garden in the island's capital, St John's.)

The Copper and Lumber Store Inn has its own waterside garden sheltering behind high walls of weathered brick. Bleached linen awnings shade a sitting area which is protected by raised stone-edged beds of mixed shrubs, subshrubs, perennials and annuals. The garden of the Admiral's Inn is also sheltered by similar raised beds. On the landward side of the inn, there is sufficient shelter to allow a pair of young traveller's trees (*Ravenala madagascariensis*) to flourish. With their huge fan-like arrangement of leaves they form a striking frame for the inn's main entrance.

English Harbour remains one of the finest examples of architectural conservation in the Caribbean, not least on account of the way in which its redevelopment has been integrated with an imaginative landscape and garden scheme.

English Harbour – Nelson's Dockyard is normally open all the time. At the time of writing the Botanic Gardens at St John's are not open to the public as so many plants were lost in a hurricane. It will take some time to restore it due to lack of funding.

GOVERNMENT HOUSE GARDENS
MONTSERRAT

Government House is situated in an elevated position overlooking the sea above Wapping Village, a few miles south of the island's capital, Plymouth. It is an unusually stately and sumptuous building, its wide verandas open to the sea breezes and the sound of the surf below. The core of the house dates from the eighteenth century but this was reconstructed and enlarged in 1908 in an expansive, highly-decorated Edwardian style which has come to represent the epitome of elegant colonial living of that period especially as it retains many of its antique furnishings and pictures inside. The newer part of the building and the

Prickly pear is used as a hedge in many of the islands.

garden were extensively damaged during Hurricane Hugo in 1989 but all is now restored.

The many-gabled and -towered exterior is painted green in deference to Montserrat's Irish heritage (many Irish families were among the island's early settlers) and the central gable sports a pinnacle in the shape of a large carved wooden shamrock, always seen silhouetted against the sky. The house is surrounded on three sides by two-storeys of white-painted verandas designed in a variety of architectural styles – classical balusters on the ground floor front, baroque-style fretwork on the floor above and rococo-style ironwork on the other two sides. This gives a rich, eclectic but hardly purist architectural effect. All round the base of the verandas has been planted a low but decorative shrubbery from which climbing plants are trained up the veranda's columns to soften the geometric lines of the house.

A curving drive descends through the garden from the elaborate iron entrance gates past a decorative sentry box – as elegant as any garden house – to end in a wide, circular carriage sweep in front of the house. The centre of the sweep is occupied by a huge flower bed, also circular, designed to be planted with annuals to give a bright colour display at all seasons of the year.

The garden around the house was designed in the form of a small park with exotic trees and shrubs, in single specimens or in groups, set apparently at random on the sloping lawns in the nineteenth-century garden style known as the 'gardenesque'. The lawns are in places interrupted by small, formally-designed garden features, for example, small fountains in a setting of low, carefully-

A splash of bright red pomegranate blossom.

crafted stone walls and areas of self-consciously arranged stone paving conceived in the then popular Arts-and-Crafts style. Set into the stones are plaques carved with commemorative or inspiring inscriptions in the sentimental manner of the time.

Many of the mature trees in the garden may have come originally from the Montserrat botanic station which had been established in 1890. The station's work was briefly interrupted in 1897 due to lack of funds. However by 1900, it was operating again with its headquarters at Grove Station, near Plymouth and with two outlying stations at Harris and Olveston respectively. By 1908, the director, Mr Robson, who had been trained at Kew, had begun to devote more space in the garden to cultivate ornamental plants as well as the economic plants which had been grown from the outset. Like the gardens of Government House, it was devastated by Hurricane Hugo but Montserrat has an ideal volcanic soil and an ideal climate for gardening. It has an ample supply of water due to the fact that both main ranges of mountains are still covered with natural forest. Humidity is low – often overnight rain clears the atmosphere. With fresh sea breezes and no marked wet and dry seasons, it is a healthy place for plants no less than for people. Since the hurricane year of 1989 many new gardens have sprung up, of which the richest in plant material is that of Mr and Mrs Crowe overlooking the golf course in Belham Valley. However, the restored gardens of Government House remain one of the most interesting survivals of an historic garden of the Edwardian period throughout the Caribbean.

> *Government House, Montserrat:* temporarily closed to the public due to volcanic activity.
> Telephone: 491–2230/8730

Gazetteer of other gardens in the Leeward Islands

BOTANIC GARDENS
ST JOHN'S, ANTIGUA

Begun in 1889, it specialised in growing dry-climate plants suitable to Antigua. The garden's activity subsequently came to a halt due to some members of the Legislative Council refusing to pay the superintendent's salary. Despite carrying on in a crippled condition, the garden boasted a large rockery by 1894 and by 1922 was seven acres in extent. Now reduced in size, it still retains plants appropriate to its water-retentive, limestone soil.

(The garden is presently closed to the public while restoration takes place after recent hurricane damage. Telephone: 462–1007/8/9)

RAWLINS PLANTATION
NEWCASTLE, ST KITTS

An eighteenth-century greathouse rebuilt by the Walwyn family in 1970, its high location on the slopes of Mount Misery ensures the benefit of the cooling breezes and adequate rainfall which are desirable for gardening. The garden acts as an integrated setting for the various plantation buildings including the eighteenth-century sugar mill and boiling house. The flamboyant tree (*Delonix regia*) is very prevalent on St Kitts and appropriately so since its

ROMNEY MANOR
ST KITTS

A plantation house, which is eighteenth century in origin, set in beautiful gardens with pleasant views over the coast. Featured is a beautiful old saman tree, *Samanea saman*, with a tall, spreading, symmetrical canopy. It is sometimes known as the rain tree due to the fern-like leaflets closing up at night thus allowing rain to fall through its canopy to the ground below.

Open Monday–Friday, 8 am to 4 pm, Saturday (November to May only) 8 am to 1 pm. Telephone: 465–6253.

Widely planted, poinciana blossom makes a spectacular sight.

alternative common name, poinciana, honours an eighteenth-century French governor of St Kitts, the Count de Poinci.

Open to hotel guests primarily.

NISBET PLANTATION INN
ST KITTS

Nisbet Plantation Inn was built on the foundations of an eighteenth-century greathouse which was once the home of Fanny Nisbet who married Lord Nelson. At the entrance to the 30-acre plantation stand the ruins of a sugar mill swathed in cassia, frangipani, poinciana and hibiscus. Between the house and the half-mile-long sandy beach extends a wide lawn bordered by a double row of stately palms backed by flamboyant trees.

Open to hotel guests only.

81

Lieutenant Caddy's picture of Brimstone Hill, St Kitts. It is an interesting example of the terrain of the island.

OTTLEY'S PLANTATION INN
ST KITTS

Around a restored eighteenth-century plantation house which is now an hotel, a 15-acre ornamental garden is being landscaped to feature a number of different plants as well as colour themes.

Open during daylight business hours of the hotel. Telephone 465–7234.

WATERWORKS ESTATE
MONTSERRAT

Still owned by the descendants of the original Irish family that settled in Montserrat in 1668, this plantation is remarkably intact in all its details including its plantation house garden.

ALEXANDER HAMILTON MUSEUM
CHARLESTOWN, NEVIS

The lava-stone house, the rebuilt birthplace in 1755 of Alexander Hamilton, the first US Secretary of the Treasury, is set in an attractive garden which contains a representative collection of Nevis' plants and trees.

Open Monday to Friday, 8 am to 4 pm. Saturday 10 am to 1 pm.

FIVE

THE WINDWARD ISLANDS

Introduction and history

The Windward Islands – Dominica, St Lucia, St Vincent and the Grenadines, and Grenada – which lie to the south of the Leeward Islands are so called because they lie in the direct path of the north-eastern trade winds. The winds result in a marked contrast between the climatic conditions prevailing on the eastern side of these islands and those prevailing on the western side. On the former side, wet and windy conditions prevail, while on the latter side a dry but sheltered environment is enjoyed. The contrast is vividly described by Patrick Leigh Fermor in his book *The Traveller's Tree*. He describes the sudden change in the landscape which was visible as his boat rounded the northern tip of the island of Grenada towards the windward side:

As we rounded the north-eastern corner of the island, the scenery changed instantaneously. The smooth sand and water were

The seagrape grows throughout the islands helping to stabilise the sandy shores.

replaced by the rough windward waves and a gusty shore from which the more luxuriant trees had retreated inland. The only growth on these bleak dunes was the sea-grape, that stubborn shrub which alone is able to resist the violence of the weather. The Trade Winds had twisted and topiarized it into innumerable fantastic shapes; growing normally on the sheltered side, the part of the bush which was exposed to the east appeared to have been shorn away in flat, slanting planes. These extraordinary contortions infect the whole coastline with a disquietingly harassed and tyrannized air, as though the landscape might all at once be blown away, leaving the traveller locked there knee deep in the wet sand like a scape goat.

Gardening climate

Almost all of the Windward Islands are of volcanic origin and have high mountains. The main determinant of gardening climate is the height of the garden above sea-level. In the high mountains the average annual rainfall can be 150 inches per year, whereas on the coast below it can be as little as 60 inches per year. In the high mountains, cold winds can prevail while in sheltered coastal areas it can be unbearably hot. All the main islands therefore have a variety of different gardening climates, as well as a diversity of different natural vegetations. The rainy season lasts from May to December approximately but even in the dry season a shower can be expected every day.

The combination of rain and tropical warmth gives to these islands a green aspect – well forested on the upper levels and extensively cultivated on the lower levels. However, the combination of rain and tropical warmth also means that an abandoned garden can deteriorate and be obliterated by encroaching vegetation in a very short time.

Gardening soils

Geologically, the Windward Islands form part of an inner arc of volcanic islands which characterise the Antilles Island chain. Their fertile soils are formed as a result of the disintegration of a variety of volcanic rocks and vary from a loose friable loam to reddish clays in the mountainous regions. The valleys and river plains boast a deep vegetable mould mixed with clay, often over a free-draining substratum of sand and gravel, allowing the region to become one of the world's biggest producers of bananas, St Vincent to become the world's largest producer of arrowroot and Grenada to produce a third of the world's nutmeg.

Advantage of the good soils has recently been taken to establish a cut flower industry such as at the Mount William Plantation on St Vincent and at the Macintosh Plantation on nearby Martinique, both of which are open to visitors.

Gardening history

The evidence of elaborate petroglyphs or prehistoric rock-carvings throughout the Windward Islands indicates the existence of strong Amerindian culture before the arrival of Christopher Columbus and subsequent European settlers. For over a century and a half after European settlement, the history of the Windward Islands was one of Franco-British rivalry for possession. For example, during that period, St Lucia was seven times occupied by the French and subsequently seven times captured by the British. This meant that the development of a long period of substantial gardening activity was delayed until the second half of the eighteenth century and the first half of the nineteenth century when the islands at last began to settle down under British rule. It also meant that when gardening did begin to develop it had a distinctly French flavour – a flavour not present in the gardens of the Virgin Islands or the Leeward Islands.

In 1763, St Vincent was ceded to Britain and, in the year after, General Robert Melville, Governor of the island, founded the present botanic garden, the first in the Western hemisphere. Although the island's repossession by the French in 1778, its cession to Britain in 1783 and the long Black Carib revolt which ended in 1796 created difficult circumstances for the new garden, it carried on its activities, making a significant contribution to Caribbean history. In 1793 it became the first garden in the region to grow the breadfruit tree. Five hundred plants were deposited there by Captain Bligh who had brought them

from Tahiti with the intention that they be distributed among the islanders.

Some plantation houses and their gardens also date from this period, such as Sans Souci, now the Prime Minister's residence, on Grenada. Grenada was returned to Britain for the last time only in 1783, soon after which the nutmeg was introduced to the island as a crop. It was so successful that it insulated the economy of the island from the worst effects of the commercial failure of the sugar crop later in the following century. French influence is also seen at the spa of Soufriere on St Lucia. Created in 1785 as a result of a grant of money from Louis XV, the spa buildings were surrounded by elegant gardens which have been revived in recent years.

The Treaty of Paris (1814) finally confirmed what are known today as the Windward Islands as a British possession. A long period of stability followed in which the activity of gardening could flourish. A new spirit of optimism was expressed, for example, in the foundation of an agricultural society on Grenada and a tree-planting society on the small island of Carriacou as reported in Bayly's *Four Years Residence in the West Indies* (1830). Henry Nelson Coleridge in his *Six Months in the West Indies* (1826) describes the productive aspect of the countryside and its plantings on the island of Dominica:

Much of the country around here is covered with coffee bushes and here and there patches of cacao. The galba is chiefly planted

The botanical garden in St Vincent is the oldest in the western hemisphere.

for fence and shade. The bois immortel is used for marking boundaries.

The bois immortelle, now usually known as the coral tree with its flame red flowers, made a spectacular marker tree in the landscape and the galba, with its fragrant flowers, is still used as a shelter tree, particularly in coastal gardens.

Charles Kingsley visited a Grenadian plantation house garden which he wrote about in 1871:

The situation of the house – the principal one of the island – to which we drove is beautiful beyond description. It stands on a knoll some 300 feet in height, commanded only by a slight rise to the north; and the wind of the eastern mountains sweeps fresh and cool through a wide hall and lofty rooms. Outside, a pleasure ground and a garden with the same flowers that we plant out in summer time at home; and behind tier on tier of green wooded hill … But opposite the drawing room window rose a candelabra Cereus thirty feet high. On the lawn in front great shrubs of red frangipani carried rose-coloured flowers which filled the air with fragrance, at the end of thick and almost leafless branches. Trees hung over them with smooth greasy stems of bright copper – which has gained the name of 'Indian skin' at least in Trinidad where we often saw them wild … We admired this and that; especially a most lovely convolvulus with purple maroon flowers; and an old hog plum – a huge tree which was striking not so much from its size as from its shape. Growing among blocks of lava, it had assumed the exact shape of an English oak in a poor soil and exposed situation: globular-headed, gnarled and stunted.

Derek Walcott, the St Lucian poet, satirised the measured order of a Caribbean botanical garden of that time in his poem *The Star-Apple Kingdom* [1979]. In it, the subject fantasises one day at dusk that he can control not only the garden itself but the life of the trees within it and the skies above it:

*He looked out from the Great House windows on
clouds that still held the fragrance of fire
he saw the Botanical Gardens officially drown
in a formal dusk, where governors had strolled
and black gardeners had smiled over glinting shears
at the lilies of parasols on the floating lawns,
the flame trees obeyed his will and lowered their wicks,
the flowers tightened their fists in the name of thrift,
the porcelain lamps of ripe cocoa, the magnolia's jet
dimmed on the one circuit with the ginger lilies
and left a lonely bulb on the verandah,
and, had his mandate extended to that ceiling
of star-apple candelabra, he would have ordered
the sky to sleep, saying, I'm tired,
save the starlight for victories, we can't afford it,
leave the moon on for one more hour, and that's it.*

Perhaps the Botanical Gardens to which he refers are those of Trinidad or of St Vincent, for each is overlooked by the island's Governor's house.

As in other parts of the Caribbean the sugar slump had dire economic effect. By 1848, of St Vincent's 100 sugar estates only twelve had resident proprietors. Subsequently, much of the sugar land throughout the Windward Islands, its soil depleted by cane, was divided one way or another into smallholdings and many islanders took up subsistence gardening and farming. As on other Caribbean islands, a

One of the exotic trees in Hope Gardens, Long John (*Triploris americana*) is a native of tropical America.

systematic attempt was made to introduce new economic plants by the establishment of botanic gardens on Dominica, Grenada and St Lucia, and through the revival of the long-established botanic garden on St Vincent.

The botanic garden on Grenada was the first to be set up. In 1886 the fourteen-acre garden in the capital Georgetown was laid out, a house for the curator was built and the first Wardian cases of new plant introductions arrived by sea from Kew Gardens in London. The gardens were ready to open to the public in the following year. The gardens also pioneered the conservation of the island's native vegetation. For example the 1895 annual report contained a protest against the rapidity with which Grenada was being denuded of trees and hoped that conservation measures would be introduced quickly. In 1912 the garden was extended to cover a rocky promontory projecting into the bay and an outlying station was established on the smaller island of Carriacou. The role of the gardens in combating plant disease was report by A W Hill in his 1912 article in the *Kew Bulletin*, 'A Visit to the West Indies':

One small tree is kept as a home for scale insects and their parasitic fungus Cephalosporum lecanium *and the leaves are distributed over the island in order to spread the fungus which has resulted in keeping the lecanium scale in check.*

The botanic station at Castries on St Lucia was the next to be established, in 1887. The site chosen was a former refuse dump in a low-lying swamp next to the harbour. The first curator was a Mr John Gray, who had started off his career as gardener to Lord Brownlow, one of the principal planters in Jamaica. Gray first came to notice when he mounted an exhibition of perfumes extracted by him from West Indian flowers which were an outstanding feature of the Jamaica Court at the Colonial-Indian Exhibition in London in 1886. On arriving on St Lucia, he began the work of reclaiming and draining the swamp and laying out and planting the grounds, but his health was severely affected by the insanitary condition of the locality in which he laboured and, after repeated bouts of illness, he died in 1895. The contribution which the garden subsequently made to the island's economy can be measured by the garden's report for 1902:

Economic and other plants to the number of 15 461, exclusive of over 2000 plants delivered free to purchasers of Crown lands in the colony, were distributed during the year. Training of young gardeners and farmers was another function undertaken by the garden when an Agricultural School was amalgamated with it.

In 1905, the curator wrote: *My full school is twenty boys: they are all resident pupils and are fed, clothed and educated free for a term varying from three to five years.*

The botanic station on Dominica, which was started in 1890, was described in detail in an article in *The Gardener's Chronicle* in 1893. One part of the description describes the shelter provided by the banana trees already on site and how the layout tried to combine the requirement to acclimatise new economic plants with that of being an ornamental garden and a public recreation ground:

The land has been laid out in plots and various economic plants are being grown … The presence of great numbers of banana trees has been availed of in starting these young plants. Each plot is 110 feet square and the parting hedges are of physic nut, Jatropha curcas, *on which it is later intended to grow* Vanilla planifolia. *Liberian and Arabian coffee, different kinds of cacao, cinnamon, limes, Chinese ginger, oranges, tangerines, mulberries, lemons, musk-okro, rubbers and other types of economic plants have been placed in these plots and the walks between have been lined with pineapples of various kinds, Egyptian cotton, nutmegs and other ornamental plants.*

The delightfully informal way in which the botanic garden was organised is illustrated by this extract:

The gates, of which only one has yet been erected, are much needed. Cows and calves, sheep and goats are at present tethered on different parts of the uncultivated parts of the garden but it requires the Curator to be constantly on the alert to prevent the abuse of this privilege. On a recent visit, I came across a goat tethered to the upright leafy spike of a young royal palm: and at the same time a fine specimen of Caryota mitis *was pointed out to me as having been eaten down by a cow which had strolled through one of the gates in passing.*

The *Kew Bulletin* of 1892 describes the St Vincent Botanic Garden as having been recently reorganised and as having been of great assistance in starting the new group of smallholders on their way: *The botanic station has proved a great success in the distribution of seeds to small proprietors – a group rapidly rising into importance by reason of the purchase of Crown lands – cash £1 per acre, and £2 on credit.*

Among the most important private gardens in the Windward Islands in the late nineteenth century was that of Dr A H Nicholls on Dominica. Author of a book called *Tropical Agriculture*, his garden held such a variety of plants that the botanic garden was initially almost entirely stocked from it. (He was also a committed natural historian and explorer. With a friend, he discovered and recorded for the first time in 1870 what is now known as the Boiling Lake in the high mountains of Dominica. The nearby mountain is called Morne Nicholls after him.)

Grenada's insulation from the worst effects of the sugar slump by reason of its early development of alternative agricultural crops was to result in the survival of many of its plantation houses and their gardens. Indeed, at the turn of the present century, new plantation houses such as Morne Fendue and Tower House, near Georgetown, were constructed using traditional materials – dark volcanic stone and mortar made of a mixture of lime and molasses.

Cotton was an important crop at one time.

Tower House was surrounded by a garden in the typical eclectic style of the time – baroque-style terraces and flights of steps combined with a modernist belvedere in cast concrete. During the 1930s, nostalgia for the elegant plantation life of the past led Europeans and Americans to acquire properties in the islands. The English portrait painter, Aubrey Davidson-Houston, acquired the house of San Antoine on St Lucia and ran it as an hotel. The American millionaire, John Archibald of the Standard Oil family, created a new plantation and house at Springfield. In 1975, he donated 950 acres of rainforest to start the Dominica National Park Service.

The post-World War II period was a time when conservation of the natural world of the Windward Islands became a priority. As a result, many National Park areas have been created. Some National Parks incorporate display gardens. An example is at the Union Nature Trail on St Lucia where there is a medical garden featuring herbs from which traditional Caribbean medical remedies are derived. The conservation of these kinds of plants received a boost with the publication in 1980 of *Caribbean Wild Plants and their Uses* by Penelope Honeychurch. It was the first attempt to list systematically and publish remedies which had been passed down orally from generation to generation throughout the Caribbean.

The gardener visiting the Windward Islands today can enjoy not only a number of contemporary gardens but also many flowers, native or naturalised throughout the countryside. The high-elevation roads of St Lucia are bordered with an attractive wild ginger which grows profusely and scents the air. Purple-flowered water hyacinths float on the

The water hyacinth growing in still water is a charming sight.

surface of Freshwater Lake on Dominica. On Grenada, cocoa plantations are shaded by tall, scarlet-flowered bois immortelle trees. The natural phenomenon of elfin woodlands – in which the trees become gnarled and miniaturised as a result of the tough conditions – can be enjoyed on high-altitude mountains. The visitor can also enjoy the

flower festivals held on St Lucia on the feast of St Rose of Lima (known as La Rose) on August 3rd of each year and on the feast of St Margaret Mary Alacoque (known as La Marguerite) on October 17th. They are especially good in the village of Mon Repos.

Of contemporary gardens which are open to the public, Bay Gardens in Grenada, a three-acre collection of tropical plants, The Spa Gardens, Soufriere in St Lucia, which have recently been revived and The Papillote Wilderness Retreat in Dominica which was begun in 1969 are among the most outstanding.

The rich heritage of gardens in the Windward Islands derives, in part, from the climate which provides abundant rainfall as well as tropical warmth but it also derives from the islands' rich cultural mix – as well as the usual European and West African influences, there is a strong French cultural presence and the only remaining Carib populations in the area.

The Caribbean suits tree ferns very well. These are at the Papillote Wilderness Retreat.

DOMINICA

Introduction

Dominica's historian Lennox Honychurch writes: *More than most islands, the environment has guided the course of Dominica's history … This environment gave the early Caribs a natural fortress against the European settlers and kept Dominica uncolonised for a longer period than the other islands.* Dominica became the last refuge of the Caribs.

Columbus sighted Dominica on his second voyage in early 1493. He did not land and sailed northwards to Marie Galante, sending a caravel to investigate the island for a safe harbour. One such was discovered on the west coast, out of view of the track other ships took. As more ships crossed the Atlantic a curious mixture of peoples ended up on Dominica. Some came there by shipwreck, some were captured in Carib raids on other islands, some were fugitives from other islands. The Caribs carried out a series of raids on the islands to the north, partly to discourage European settlement and in particular to try to stop it spreading any further south. They were able to return to Dominica and take refuge from reprisals high in their closely wooded mountains.

Dominica was first landfall from Europe and trade began between the Europeans and the Caribs. There were peaceful visits from passing ships when *plantains, pinas and potatoes* were traded for *hatchets, knives and small beads.* The traders were also able to renew their supplies of water and

firewood. The usual crops grown by the Caribs were plantains, potatoes, pinas (pineapples), papaya, pumpkins, calabash, peppers, mammee apples, guavas, tobacco and cotton. By the middle of the sixteenth century they were also growing sugar-cane.

Relations between French and English were no better than they had ever been by the last quarter of the seventeenth century. The only idea they had in common seemed to be the subduing of the Caribs in St Vincent and Dominica. This neither of them could achieve and by 1686 it was agreed that the two islands should be left for the exclusive use of the Caribs. This resolve did not last long and soon small settlements of lumbermen were to be found on the coast. The warring and raiding had had an effect on the numbers of Caribs: in 1647 there had been 5000 of them, by 1730 there were only 400 left.

Gardening climate

Dominica has a climate which is suitable for an agricultural system based largely on tree crops whose roots bind the soil. The island lies about 15.5° north of the Equator and is in the path of the south equatorial current which flows from West Africa to South America, and then into the Caribbean sea. Dominica is around 29 miles long and 16 miles wide, with a high backbone of mountains running along the centre from north to south. These mountains cut across the path of the north-east trade winds that sweep in from the Atlantic. The winds are forced upwards before they reach the mountains and moist air and heavy clouds are formed out at sea and over the east coast. The rain therefore falls along the windward side of the island and heavily in the mountains. By the time the air reaches the leeward side it has lost most of its moisture – what is known as the 'rain shadow' effect. The amount of rainfall varies from 50 inches on the dry west coast to 300 inches per annum in the mountains. February and March are the driest months and July the wettest. June is the hottest at 20°C to 32°C, January the coolest at 20°C to 29°C. The climatic conditions have affected the varieties of forest which grow on Dominica. On the east and north coasts there is windward littoral forest, which includes swamp forest in the north. The west coast has dry scrub woodland. Between 500 and 2000 feet on the east and 1000 to 2000 feet on the west there is tropical rainforest, with seasonal, deciduous woodland lower down. Higher up is the montane or cloud forest with elfin woodland around the highest peaks.

Gardening soils

Dominica is of volcanic origin with several dormant volcanoes and at least four that are thought to be active. Volcanic activity threw up the mountain ranges and erosion has broken down the steep rock formations and dug out the deep valleys. Landslides are a frequent occurrence after heavy rain, and swollen rivers continue to break down the banks and sweep away the soil. The richest areas of soil are in the bottom of valleys and along the coast. Here the big plantations were built while small farmers scratched a living from the thinner soils along the ridges and mountainsides. Rivers brought down alluvial deposits to form narrow valleys opening out on to the sea shore.

Gardening history

Dominica became an island of the small planter and farmer, without large sugar estates or hundreds of slaves. The landholdings were small and mostly worked by the owners with little assistance. These owners were not rich but they were independent. They grew coffee, cotton, cocoa and tobacco, plus provisions for the slaves on the larger islands. The other islands also provided them with a market for the wood they cut. The growing of sugar was discouraged by the bigger islands.

Few slaves were brought directly to Dominica and those that did arrive were usually house slaves and personal servants. The French passed a *Code Noir* in 1685 and this governed the conditions for slaves. It regulated the sale and ownership of them, limited punishment and laid down minimum conditions for feeding and housing. It also laid down rules for training them and even for their baptism as Christians.

This appears to have had some good influence on the relationship between slaves and masters. The slaves were provided with basic clothes, food and small houses which were thatched and built of mud. They also got small plots of land on which they could grow provisions, raise chickens and pigs and thereby make themselves a little extra at

A view of the restored garden at Ridgefield.

the Sunday markets. Occasionally enough money could be made to buy their freedom. But not all men and women of colour in Dominica were slaves. Many mulatto people had come from other islands and they formed a plantocracy of their own. They owned estates and did join some professions although others were barred to them.

The Seven Years War of 1756 to 1763 affected Dominica, as it did the other islands of the Caribbean, with various naval engagements off its shores and the British invasion of the island. As British settlement increased surveyors and map-makers were sent out from the home country. The land in Dominica was divided into lots though very little attention was paid to the actual lie of the land except for the extremely precipitous slopes and deep valleys. The lots were auctioned off in England, unseen by the buyers, and the confusion was absolute. There were no roads and money would have to be spent on them before any farm or estate buildings could be raised. Many buyers were speculators who had no intention of coming out, but sent their attorneys and overseers to run the estates. In all this confusion a mere 232-acre plot was assigned to the Caribs.

There is a very good account of Dominica in 1776 by Joseph Stenhouse. His family were involved with trade in Barbados and he was appointed in 1771 to be Collector and Comptroller of Customs in Roseau by the patron of the family, Sir James Lowther. Stenhouse went to Dominica in 1771 and then again in 1776, never to return. The first social change he remarks on is that by that date there was a Lieutenant-Governor, a Collector, a Judge, a Solicitor-General and a white community plus the 70th Regiment quartered there. He and two friends undertook an expedi-

tion to the lake up in the mountains. Stenhouse gives a vivid description of the steep valleys and thick vegetation to be seen on the way, saying he could not imagine the sun ever reaching the bottom of the valleys. The path, being extremely slippery, was quite terrifying on horseback and one wretched horse disappeared down a ravine. His rider threw himself off in the nick of time. There were also large trees that had fallen across the tracks but he noted the tree ferns and the festooning grey moss. As they climbed higher towards the lake the trees *dwindled almost into shrubs generally not more than twelve or thirteen feet high and surrounded with a thick coat of moss.* The lake had fish in it and the air was blissfully cool and fresh. A wonderful view was to be had with the rain storms over parts of the island below them. For part of the return journey Stenhouse and his companions decided to walk, leading their horses as a more secure way of transport. They visited two plantations, one belonging to a Colonel O'Hara which was near the *large, limpid River of Rosalie* which had a good bridge over it. The estate boasted a hospital, the building itself seeming more handsome than the dwelling house, and there was a Prussian surgeon. The other estate belonged to Colonel Bruce and had to be approached by canoe. On the short journey they saw large flocks of several different kinds of birds, including tropic birds nesting in the cliffs. This estate was reckoned to be one of the best in Dominica, producing 200 hogsheads of sugar. It too had a swift-running river to drive its mill. He also describes a most elaborate waterwheel which could be used instead of the mill. The only disadvantage was that the river was liable to devastating floods, the last having been in 1774, but it had good fish in it, including crayfish and lobsters. He must have swum in the river because he says *to bathe in a Tropical climate in so fine a stream as this, an exercise I have frequently indulged myself in, is a luxury not be described and to be fully known must be felt.*

By the last quarter of the eighteenth century Dominica was beginning to develop some of the same characteristics of the other islands. Ships were arriving with loads of slaves and plantations were growing coffee and sugar. There were still no good roads and schooners travelled the coast carrying mail, food and merchandise to the isolated settlements. These same schooners then collected the sugar and coffee for export. It was a lonely life for the managers of the plantations and some complained bitterly of the climate as well. The managers' houses on the plantations were not as grand or elaborate as they were in Jamaica or Barbados. As they were only for managers, the owners saw no good reason to spend extra money, but the houses had the usual good proportions and charm of the eighteenth century.

Between 1775 and 1812, Dominica, like the other Caribbean islands, was much affected by the wars between Britain and her American colonies, and Britain and France. Dominica was under French control for five years, during which there were several disasters. In 1779 and 1780 there were terrible hurricanes which destroyed buildings and crops and killed livestock. In 1781 Roseau was destroyed by fire. Then the Maroons, runaway slaves, some of them descendants of those who had run away a century before to live with the Caribs, began to rebel. They lived up in the security of the mountains where no one could reach them

Lieutenant Caddy's picture of Roseau, Dominica. It gives a good impression of the towering, tree-covered terrain.

because of the difficult terrain and lack of roads. They continued their insurrection until they were at last brought under control by the troops sent by the Governor. The war of 1812, when America again declared war against the British, caused disruption of food supplies to Dominica and there was a series of devastating hurricanes. A letter from the manager of one estate sums up the situation: *The shingles were stripped off the east of the dwelling house and part of the east end of the boiling house roof fell in. The hospital, horse stable, wood and timber house blown down as well as several of the Negro houses … Canes twisted and twirled about and most of them laid flat and an almost entire destruction of the provision grounds … At present the island is destitute of rice, flour, biscuits, corn meal or in fact any sort of eatables. We shall be obliged to feed the Negroes three or four months, regardless of the expense or inconvenience.* The peace treaty was signed in 1814 but it took some time before supplies were back to normal. All this had the effect that any planters who could emigrated to promising new colonies – Trinidad and Demarara.

In 1825 yet another devastating hurricane hit the island and we have a sad account of the state of the island after it. *Mills, works and dwellings are destroyed, canes lodged or torn up, Coffee Estates almost deprived both of their old and young plants, some pieces completely washed away and their buildings blown down … plantain walks ruined, fruit and other trees destroyed and the country round those parts looking as if a fire had gone through it and blasted it … The noted fine large Tamarind Tree, under whose shady boughs the Market has been held for years, having been planted according to tradition, a century or two back, was torn up by the roots.*

Another visitor that year, referring to Roseau remarked: *All was silent and soft and lifeless like a city in the Arabian Nights … the grass grows lush and verdantly between the stones … there is no public voice to call forth or public encouragement to support the exertion of individual virtue and talent; the community is divided by language, by religion … the mere routine of government was at a dead stand while I was on the island.*

In the year 1834 the abolition of slavery was finally enacted by the British Government. The disorder that had been expected did not take place. At first an apprenticeship scheme was launched for the freed slaves in an effort to accustom them to total freedom and to help the planters with the problem of labour. The apprentices were to receive the same benefits as they had had before, such as shelter, clothing, medical attention and food, but in spite of this it was not a success and the scheme had to be abandoned. The British owners of plantations were often absentee landlords and the estates were run by their attorneys whereas the French plantations were usually owner-occupied and they looked after their slaves better, even teaching the labourers themselves. This must have contributed to the better relationship between the French and their slaves.

The fact was that there was spare land in abundance in Dominica and the freed slaves were able to set up their own smallholdings so setting the pattern for the future of small independent farmers. In other islands where there were large sugar plantations very often there was no spare land and the ex-slaves were forced to return to the plantations to earn a living for themselves. The problem of labour for the estates still remained. It was solved in other islands by the importation of labour from China and India but this did not happen in Dominica. A few Portuguese came as part of their migrations of the nineteenth century but that was all. This caused a radical social change and some of the large estates were broken up, and some were abandoned to be taken over in small lots by the newly freed coloured people.

During the next fifty years the island's sugar cultivation almost ceased and arrowroot and cassava became the main cash crops, but there were still no roads over the island except those that had existed in the eighteenth century, and these were really only paths. Goods had still to be carried round to Roseau by boat which presented certain dangers.

Victorian observers, in particular Anthony Trollope, writing in 1860, did not have a high opinion of what they saw: *Every house is in a state of decadence. There are no shops that can properly so be called. The people wander about idle, chattering, listless, there is no sign of money made or of money making ... Everything seems to speak of desolation, apathy, ruin.*

Luckily for Dominica two remarkable men came to the island, both as doctors and both with a strong interest in botany and plants. They explored the island and documented many plants that had not been officially discovered before. The first to arrive was Dr John Imray who came to assist his brother, also a doctor. He did a great deal of work on the tropical diseases of the day such as malaria, yellow fever and yaws.

It was Dr Imray who introduced Liberian coffee to Dominica and also the lime which was to prove of such enormous economic benefit to the island. In 1873 Dr Alford

Arrowroot is one of the main crops of Dominica.

Nicholls arrived. He was already interested in tropical agriculture and he started to propagate and cultivate certain crops. He was in correspondence and contact with the Royal Botanical Gardens at Kew and, in exchange for plants of interest from Dominica, Kew sent him possible useful economic plants for trial in the island. Dr Nicholls also corresponded with other men interested in the flora of the islands and was responsible for sending plants to the St Vincent Botanic Gardens.

By the 1880s alarm was being felt and expressed by the British Government as to the economic fortunes of the West Indian islands and it was acknowledged that help was needed. A scheme was suggested whereby a network of botanical gardens and stations should be set up throughout the islands. The purpose of these was both to provide seeds and plants for the local farmers and to set up agricultural teaching establishments for the training of local youths in the knowledge of farming. These establishments were graded according to the area under cultivation and the qualifications of the officer in charge. Thus a botanic department was under the charge of a director

The nursery is one of the most important features of a botanic garden.

with superintendents under him. The area under cultivation might be between 100 to 300 acres. A botanic garden seldom had more than 50 acres under cultivation and a botanic station was more modest, usually under the direction of a highly trained gardener with anything from three to 30 acres. Royal Commissions were appointed in 1882 and in 1896, and it was as a direct result of these that the network of botanical establishments were set up. Dominica got its garden laid out and started in 1890. Within a few years there was an agricultural school at Morne Bruce which was much appreciated by the local young men. The next thirty years seem to have been the high spot for local agriculture. A dynamic Administrator, Mr Hesketh Bell, encouraged this with many new ideas both as to crops which he grew on his own estate, which was run as an experimental farm, and his insistence on a new road being built right through the centre of the island so opening up large areas of farming land not available before.

Sugar cultivation continued in a small way and coffee was also still grown and exported but cocoa had largely replaced coffee and limes accounted for a large area. The British firm of Rowntrees owned three cocoa estates and Rose's Lime Juice Company had a large factory on the edge of Roseau. Oranges, coconuts, spices, cassava, vanilla, pineapples and other fruits were also grown for export to both America and Britain.

The first World War had another devastating effect on trade to and from Dominica There was a lack of shipping and Dominica was thrown back on her own resources as well as sending her menfolk to fight. Hurricanes lashed her in 1915, 1916 and 1917. The one of 1916 was the worst and damaged crops and trees, livestock and homes and even swept away the roads on the west coast. After the war was over the lime trade started up again but after a few years the trees were struck with two diseases, one that of withering tip the other which attacked the trunk of the trees. Experts were rushed from Britain and Trinidad to help. It was decided to try grafting on to the common citrus stock, a method which was successful and has had to be used in other islands to avoid sweet orange diseases. Sadly though, time was not on Dominica's side; Sicily was growing lemons and modern methods were producing citric acid by other means. Once again fresh suggestions were made for new and different crops, this time coconuts and bananas.

These two crops have proved to be the staples for Dominica ever since. Other crops are grown but the trade in bananas still continues. Coconuts are exported to Barbados and Trinidad to be refined into oil and fat products. Grapefruit was a new crop and the lime factories could be used to process it. Bay leaf and oil are other crops and coffee and cocoa are still grown in small quantities. The large estates have declined and Dominica is now a nation of small farmers. One of the good things to happen is the advent of eco-tourism and Dominica has become the mecca for those interested in personally walking her mountain ways and experiencing her unique beauty and fascination.

Gardens

✾ THE BOTANIC GARDENS ✐
ROSEAU

The Botanic Gardens were developed as part of the network of such gardens and stations throughout the Caribbean. In 1885, Sir Joseph Hooker, then Director of Kew Botanic Gardens in England, expressed the opinion that there could be no doubt that the future prosperity of the West Indies would be largely affected by the extension to other islands of the same facilities as then existed in Jamaica. Jamaica at that time was sending seeds and cuttings and plants to other islands in the Caribbean to help them extend the range of plants they grew.

The *Kew Bulletin* of 1888 contained an interesting passage in which it was pointed out that because of droughts in other islands, Dominica was the nearest fruit growing island to the USA, Canada and Great Britain. Many fruit trees grew spontaneously; there were in fact sixty different kinds of fruit grown and there was aready considerable trade between Dominica and the other islands. Expansion of this trade was urged and it was noted that at last the planters were turning their attention to deliberate planting of fruit trees. Of these fruits, lime was the most important and was exported in the form of juice.

It was announced that an establishment of a botanical garden or station would facilitate the flow of information and advice. It was also said that the island was *admirably situated within the tropics with a broken and varied surface with*

Some of the avocado and citrus trees in the citrus nursery beds.

its sheltered valleys and steep mountainsides and not much more than one tenth of the land under cultivation. So it was that in 1890 the garden was started.

Dr Daniel Morris, who had been working in Jamaica, was appointed to be the Commissioner in charge of the botanical gardens of the Caribbean. He went on a personal tour of many of the islands and so was present at the laying out of the garden on a site which he thought appropriate. It consisted of 40 acres which he considered would be good growing land. There is a description of its position. *The Botanic Station lies at the back of the town of Roseau on slightly elevated land about half a mile from the sea. Its situation is romantic. Immediately to the east rise the steep cliffs of Morne Bruce to a height of five to six hundred feet above the sea level. Paths cut along the sides of these cliffs form delightful shady walks while the sun's rays are still in the east and plenty of trees and bamboo clumps will render them equally enjoyable in the latter half of the day. The station lies mapped out below and as new beds and roads are being laid out the appearance of the whole is very attractive ... picturesque glimpses may be had up the Roseau valley.* The emphasis was always on the fact the gardens had been established for growing economic and commercial plants.

Mr Joseph Jones was the superintendent of the gardens in 1892 and he has left a detailed report on the state of the gardens at that date. There had been a gap between the last superintendent's resignation and Mr Jones' arrival, and he complained about the state of the garden due to lack of supervision, but his description of the amount of work that had been done is breathtaking – the sheer volume of plants put out, the levelling of land which proved to be stony and dry, the laying out of a carriage road through the gardens, one hundred yards by twenty-five feet wide which was *macadamised and covered with terras,* the improvement of paths and bridging of drains. He describes how the nursery area, which he regards as the most important part, had been hedged with annatto (*Bixa orellana*).

Plants raised in pots waiting to be distributed.

The plants he raised had a ready sale. Amongst these were limes, oranges, cacao, coffee, cola nuts, vines, nutmegs and cloves. He had also introduced the tree tomato and the cherimoyer to the island. Some of the land was even drier and stonier than other parts and on these he grew sisal hemp (*Agave rigida*) and sansevieria. Cacao plants of the Montserrat variety did very well and commanded a good price. Liberian coffee also did well but cinnamon was difficult to establish because he considered the soil was too light. Nutmeg was not easy to establish but cloves were doing well. The physic nut (*Jatropha curcas*), which was used as the host plant for the vanilla orchid and Siamese ginger (*Alpinia galanga*) absolutely flourished. He was very pleased that a durian tree, the seed of which he obtained from Dr Nicholls, was doing well and thought it was the first time it had fruited in the West Indies (it is a native of the Far East). A mangosteen had been sent out from Kew as well.

In spite of this apparently optimistic picture a report appeared in the *Gardeners' Chronicle* in August of 1893 by Mr C A Banber, Superintendent of Agriculture, in which he said: *The site selected for the botanic station is not all that could be desired. As a general rule it has been thought proper that where new and beautiful plants are being grown, they should be placed near a large town where the largest population is concentrated. But the real purpose of a botanic station has frequently been lost sight of and the attempt to combine a public recreation ground with an acclimatisation garden has crippled the work of the more useful and less ornamental character.*

This is a problem that has been, and still is, one for many botanical gardens and stations. Public use can be very destructive, especially on a garden's lawns.

In the garden at present there are no goats or cows but there is a great deal of public use and which adds to difficulties of maintenance. The West Indies Commission Report of 1897 noted, however, that in the six years of its existence the gardens had distributed 165 000 economic plants and the cost of the station was £400 while the net receipts were £99. It was hoped to extend the work of the station, employ agricultural instructors and establish an industrial school for local pupils.

The garden today still has its original layout with a carriage road winding through the centre of the garden and gates in place. Its purpose is still to propagate economic plants for the island. There are other small stations all over Dominica but the Botanic Garden has an additional purpose today in that it propagates ornamental plants for the new housing and landscaping schemes. There is a particular emphasis on plants from tropical South America and Eastern Asia. To the west of the main carriageway are the administrative buildings and beyond, in a shallow valley lying below Morne Bruce, are the square beds laid out as in many other botanic gardens. The economic and ornamental plants are divided by a hedge of sweet lime (*Triphasia trifolia*) which when crushed in the hand gives off a sweet scent. The original upper and lower paths are still there, the upper being reached by a flight of 35 steps and winding past the native species area. In the nursery more cuttings are used these days than seeds except for palms. At one time there were more than a hundred species of palms in the gardens but the devastation of hurricanes has sorely depleted their number.

Up the slope beyond the propagating beds there are parrot houses where the two types of native parrot are being reared, both endangered species. The red-necked parrots, known as 'jackos', of which there are only about 500 left in the wild, are accompanied by sisseron parrots, which are even more endangered. The numbers of parrots are increasing, but many birds get killed during hurricanes.

There are no hibiscus in the gardens, which is not noticeable because there is so much else, but the hibiscus became diseased and had to be removed. An orchid project was launched in an effort to persuade the farmers to develop an export trade in orchids. The native orchid *Epidendrum ciliare* is used and dendrobiums and vandas were brought in. *Oncidium altissimum*, which has a tiny yellow with maroon flower, were obtained. These are grown on a medium of charcoal and stone which has the advantage of being easily available.

In spite of the recent spate of very destructive hurricanes, including the one in 1979 which blew a large baobab tree across a bus, which is still there, there are still many very handsome trees in the gardens. The official guide to the garden gives a very good map of the layout and a list of the trees. Many of the trees line the main carriageway while others stand on the cricket pitch west of the main gate. Just inside the Roseau Gate the trees start and there is an ylangylang (*Cananga odorata*), a native of tropical Asia which is used in the making of perfume. Close to it is the often-planted frangipani (*Plumeria acuminata*) a native of tropical America and a *Bauhinia variegata* or orchid tree with flowers of white, light mauve or deep purple which originates in South-East Asia. The *Podocarpus coriaceus* is a native and back against the hedge are Bermuda cedars (*Juniperus bermudiana*). They have attractive blue berries in season. Further on trees line both sides of the road and amongst them is a balata (*Manilkara bidentata*) known locally as the bullet tree from the hardness of its wood. It also produces a useful latex, and is another native of tropical America. Nearby is a *Brownea grandiceps*, which has brilliant scarlet flowers, and a pride of Burma (*Amherstia nobilis*) which grows well in the West Indies although it is not widely planted. At the junction is an amusing feature – a bamboo circle which is hollow in the centre. I was told it was used as a private place for courting couples. In one early description of the garden there was a proposal to have a lily pond here with the water-lily *Victoria amazonica*. Dotted about the lawns are some of the usual shrubs seen in gardens like allamanda (*A. cathartica*) and oleander (*Nerium oleander*), crotons in their different yellows and reds, as well as bougainvillea and ixora. There is also a flamboyant tree (*Delonix regia*) and on the far side of the cricket pitch is what would appear to be its yellow cousin as the flowers look so similar. In fact it is *Peltophorum pterocarpum* from Indo-Malaysia.

Various fruit trees are still grown in the gardens. The spices – nutmeg (*Myristica fragrans*), clove and pimento plus the starfruit or carambola – are there. There are grafted orange trees using sour orange stock. The avocado trees are still there but there used to be more of the old species and there were exotic and different types of mango, but these too have gone. Unfortunately the necessary

The renewed palm avenue.

financing for replanting is not available although the costs would not be overly high.

As one walks towards the Elmshall Gate there are more interesting trees to be seen: a newly started palm avenue and a mahogany avenue consisting of *Swietenia mahagoni* and *Swietenia macrophylla*. Then there is the bitter bark (*Colvillea racemosa*) and the cannonball tree (*Couroupita guianensis*), an unusual sight with the fruit coming straight from the trunk and all the leaves at the top of the tree. The velvet tamarind has its place and round the cricket pitch can be seen saman trees (*Samanea saman*) and neem trees (*Azadirachta indica*). Neem trees in India are much valued, not only for their shade and timber, but also for their medicinal properties, and its use as an insecticide.

These gardens are still very worthwhile visiting. It is sad so much has been lost in hurricanes but sadder still that the money to maintain them does not seem to be available. So much good work is still being done here for the people of Dominica with all the ideals and purpose of the original founders and so much was done in the past. It seems a shame that with the widespread concept of plant species preservation more money could not be allotted to Dominica's unique heritage of plants.

Gardens open every day between 6.00 am and 7.00 pm.
(Open on moonlit nights 6.00 am to 10.00 pm.)

D'AUCHAMPS GARDENS

The D'Auchamps Estate belongs to the well-known Dominican Honychurch family. Mr Lennox Honychurch is an historian and is very knowledgeable about his island. His sister Sara is as well known as a gardener. The estate is typical of an old family estate except possibly it is smaller being only nine acres with four of those for the garden. The house is a fairly new one and recently an annexe has been added to accommodate paying guests. Ms Sara Honychurch has decided to open the garden to tourists and extend it to give it several themes. One is to grow the useful and edible plants that are so often mentioned in the Caribbean but not recognised by visitors, another to have two beds, at least, of medicinal tea plants and to divide the garden into shade and sun areas. She also wants a wooded area where native plants which have been brought in from the bush can grow. She has had a small plant nursery for some years and so she is well qualified for her new venture.

The garden is on the same road as Papillote Wilderness Retreat that winds up from Roseau to Trafalgar Falls. It is on the steep hillside but not in quite as steep an area as Papillotte. Presumably the original builders chose the spot for its slightly flatter terrain. There is a car-park at the entrance marked by clumps of large bamboos. The drive winds up to the house past a large lawn and some of the original native forest trees. Hidden behind this screen of

The entrance to the D'Auchamps garden, showing the house and lawn.

trees in a circular walk which starts at the site of the original nursery, now the sunny area. Here are the ticket booth and a sitting area for the fruit drink or tea you will enjoy after your walk. This also acts as the stock area having various ornamental shrubs and different coleus. It is a garden in itself with small paths. Then a path turns down towards the useful and edible plant area. The bank on the hillside is covered with anthuriums. Anthuriums have become a commercially important ornamental plant and are now grown widely in the Caribbean for export. In particular *A. andraeanum* and its cultivars and hybrids (*A. carneum*, *A. cultorum*, *A. ferrerense* and *A. andraeanum* 'Guatemala'). There is an amazing range of colours from pure white through all the shades of red to crimson. They are epiphytes and like half-shade such as is provided by this bank and the large trees above. On the right of the path is to be found dasheen (*Colocasia esculenta*), cassava (*Manihot esculenta*), tannia, passion fruit, (*Passiflora edulis*) and other produce for the table. Dasheen, as well as having an edible root, has an edible green top used for the excellent soup 'Callaloo' so often encountered in Dominica. Cassava is also a root which used to be dried, ground, washed and made into a type of flour for making a porridge or for baking. Tannia is a root rather similar to an eddoe which is potato-like in its consistency and taste. *Aloe vera* has found its way here too although it is a medicinal plant. Further on you come upon great stands of heliconia (there are eight or nine varieties) and ginger plants, both the pink and the shell ginger. There is an ylangylang tree (*Cananga odorata*)

Part of the stock area for plants.

here too, part of the original planting of the estate. An opening has been cut in the screen of trees and under a large *Ficus citrifolia* you may sit on a bench and look out to the Trafalgar Falls and the valley below you, with the mountains on the other side.

Then the path opens out into the orchard area. Here you will find soursop (*Annona muricata*), cocoa (*Theobroma cacao*), mango (*Mangifera indica*) and different varieties of bananas and plantains (*Musa* sp.), sugar-cane (*Saccharum officinarum*) and tobacco. Because it is sheltered there is also a trellis with a christophine vine (*Sechium edule*) on it. There are pawpaw trees (*Carica papaya*), avocado (*Persea americana*) and different yams (*Dioscorea* sp.) and beds of medicinal plants for bush teas. There are also small trees of Barbados cherry (*Malphigia emarginata*), a fruit used for jam, and guava (*Psidium guajava*) plus pumpkins (*Cucurbita* sp.) and sweet potato (*Ipomoea batatas*). The idea is that it should be like a village garden. There are plants here that are no longer found in a village garden such as both the red and white arrowroot (*Maranta arundinacea*), topi tambo, which looks like a small potato but tastes like a Jerusalem artichoke and the wild raspberry. The background to all this is the citrus orchard containing grapefuit, orange and lime trees.

From this scene of plenty the path turns again into the woodland, a shady and semi-shady area. Here and there are wild ferns and wild begonias brought in from the forest and some wild creepers make their way up the trees. Pileas help to provide ground cover. As the visitor makes his or her way out into the sunlight again they pass a clump of tropical iris, including the yellow and blue and white-flowered forms.

It is planned to devote the area near the entrance to spice trees. There will be bay, allspice, clove and room will also be made for coffee, mammee (*Mammea americana*) (which produces a large round brown fruit tasting like a cross between a pear and a peach), sapodilla (*Manilkara zapota*) (a sweet brown fleshed fruit with black seeds), carambola, pomerac, ackee (*Blighia sapida*), which is the national fruit of Jamaica and tastes like scrambled egg, and both breadfruit (*Artocarpus altilis*) and breadnut. Already the estate has nutmeg (*Myristica fragrans*) and cinnamon (*Cinnamomum zeylanicum*) and there are coconuts in the garden.

This is a unique idea and a unique garden and most interesting to visit. A very good map is available at the gardens.

Open to the public 8.30 am to 2.30 pm.
For appointments, telephone 448–3346

PAPILLOTE WILDERNESS RETREAT

The road from Roseau winds up from the town, past where the old plantations for limes used to be (now built over) in the valley, across a bridge over the Roseau river and then creeps along the mountainside, gradually rising all the time. Always one is surrounded by the lush rainforest growth. The road passes through two small villages clinging to the mountainside and, still climbing, makes for the Trafalgar Falls. Just below the falls there is now a hydroelectric station and because of this the road is maintained to a good standard. Beside the station you come to the entrance of the enchantment that is Papillote Wilderness Retreat.

Originally this piece of land was given to some slaves to farm after the abolition of slavery and this accounts for the breadfruit trees and the coconuts which form part of the basic planting of the hillside. The view from Papillote's restaurant and its veranda is of an incredible lushness. It is a mixture of the native trees of Dominica such as flame of the forest (its French name is chataigner) (*Sloanea* sp.), which flowers orange in February, silk cotton trees (*Ceiba pentandra*), bananas, African tulip trees (*Spathodea campanulata*) and huge ginger plants.

The owner of this lovely place, Papillote, is Mrs Anne Jno Baptiste. An American by birth, from New York and Florida, she came to Dominica in 1961 and fell in love with it: the mountains, the lushness, the rivers, the panoramic

One of the several pools.

views. She started by buying a piece of land and erecting a small building to sell lemonade to the tourists. Meanwhile she had started on her garden and married her husband Cuthbert, a Dominican. The area of the garden, being part of the hillside, is in fact extremely steep. Above the cliff face which is its limit in one direction is a small plateau and from this descend two rivers or big streams. One of these is a hot mineral spring, the water of which is a strange orange colour. The other is of the lovely clarity of very pure water. Because of the denseness of the native growth there is a lot of shade in this garden and this is carefully controlled each year by cutting back the bigger trees like the breadfruit (*Artocarpus altilis*) with its large leaves. Areas had to be cleared to make an open meadow area, the witches' garden and space for the fruit trees and vegetables grown for the restaurant and hotel.

Mrs Baptiste is above all an environmentalist and knowledgeable gardener. She pays a lot of attention to the enrichment of the soil, mulching and composting. With such a high rainfall (the average is 250 inches a year) and the resulting leaching of the soil this is very important. The growth rate is phenomenal. However when Hurricane David arrived in 1979 all her previous work was swept away. The whole valley was scoured of its soil, its trees and its plants. For a year afterwards, Mrs Baptiste could not look up at the hillsides without tears coming to her eyes at such monumental destruction. But she started again, rebuilding walls, making paths, planning, planting. As she says, 'I was young and full of energy.' The hurricane had taken the deep shade so different planting was possible – a hopeful view so many gardeners have to take at difficult

Spring water issues from the mouth of a fantastic stone fish-like creature.

times. The buildings also had to be reconstructed. This has really only just been completed. There is now a reception area, restaurant-kitchen plus a small shop for local crafts. It is from here one gets the marvellous sweeping view that gives a very good idea of both the lushness of growth of Dominica and also of its rejuvenation powers. It is also from here that the visitor can look down on the last of the hot spring pools which has a calabash (*Crescentia cujete*) growing near and leaning over the pool. Further up the hillside there is a building containing bedrooms known as the rainforest rooms and from here one looks out and feels a very part of that rainforest.

Further up again is an administration building, with a space for chairs to sit in. Under this building is the first of the hot pools. This pool is fed by a spring issuing from the mouth of a huge stone fish, similar to a fanciful grouper. In the garden there are many of these animal sculptures, made by a Canadian who came to stay for a few weeks. By now they are so covered by moss and ferns, so much part of the landscape that it is not easy to spot them at first. Visitors may bath in this pool. It is about four feet deep with side shelves. As one sits looking up into the surrounding greenery it feels as if one is in the original Eden. There is a realisation that everything grows on everything else. There is an orange tree with its fruits and bromeliads hanging from its branches. On its trunk there are orchids (the local ones, *Maxillaria coccinea*). The tree ferns (*Cyathea arborea*) have more bromeliads and other small ferns are growing on them. The palms are covered by ferns and orchids and the local orchids have small flowers of lime green and white, some red.

It is here too that Mrs Baptiste has her 'potting shed', where the propagation goes on. Her crowd of small pots are to be seen all round. She goes to many plant shows all over America and Canada and also gets seed from various plant societies. She brings in cuttings and plants from the 'bush'. Like all enthusiastic gardeners she is still planning

parts of the garden, still extending. Her latest enthusiasm is to extend her orchid collection and she has just acquired a couple of hundred locally made orchid containers. Because of the high humidity orchids grow well but in a very small amount of growing medium. She has *Epidendrum ciliare* amongst others.

There are some plants she particularly likes and the garden is planted into areas for collections of species. There are collections of gingers, bromeliads, aroids, alocasias, ferns, begonias and heliconias. Small paths wind throughout the garden going up and down the hillside. They cross the hot and cold streams, travel up to the waterfall and down to the third hot pool, on to the fruit and vegetable gardens and to the witches' garden where local medicinal plants and herbs are grown. These paths are now being concreted and steps are being made to make access easier. One of the paths leads up to the chicken house where there are no ordinary chickens but exotic be-wigged, be-spatted characters that the visitors will also meet on their wanderings. There are several species plus peafowl and guinea fowl. There are planters round the buildings and these are filled with begonias of various types, one of Mrs Baptiste's favourites, mostly raised from seed. Begonias also seed themselves in steps, in walls and anywhere they can get a foothold. Soon the new steps and paths will have their share. She has collected the indigenous varieties which have hybridised to produce several cultivars. She is propagating some endangered species from the United States, where they are difficult to grow outside rainforest conditions, and from Panama where they are dying from excessive sunlight because of the felling of the rainforest. She has

111

the cane-like superbas and the giant nelumbifolias. There is a collection of twelve different ferns plus three different tree ferns, one of them the spiky tree fern (*Cyathea imrayana*) the others *C. arborea* and *C. tenera*. Bromeliads also do extremely well and there is *Aechmea smithiorum* and *Guzmania plumieri*. There is a most splendid and exotic jade vine (*Strongylodon macrobotrys*) hanging in the shade of an orange tree; apparently jade vines do well on citrus. Anthuriums do very well in Dominica also. The 'mibi' anthurium (*A. palmatum*) was used by the Caribs for basket making. *A. hookeri* is there and there is a *A. dominicense* from the area of the island's Boiling Lake, its fine green spathe smaller than the *A. grandifolium*. The big *A. cristellanum* is there too. There is an indigenous heliconia, *H. caribaea*, which is yellow and also a yellow and peach *H. wagneriana*. There is also a South American *H. rostrata*.

The background planting to all this is a mixture of cocoa (*Theobroma cacao*), coffee, both *C. robusta* and *C. arabica* which is smaller, mammee apple (*Mammea americana*), breadfruit (*Artocarpus altilis*) and white cedar (*Tabebuia pallida*) and occasionally very large calabash (*Crescentia cujete*), and there is underplanting not yet mentioned. There is a maranta (*Ischnosiphon arouma*) which is a reed, also like the mibi anthurium used in basket-making. Aeschynanthus creeper with its red flowers makes it way up the larger trees. There is *Alocasia cuprea* with its big leaf with a red back and lower still are the creeping pileas, both red and white. On descending a path from the second hot

There are many bromeliads in this garden.

pool, the visitor will find the variegated hibiscus *H. rosasinensis 'Cooperii'* lining the path under the tree ferns. There are also gingers, most of them having a medicinal use, pink 'torch' ginger (*Etlingera elatior*), shell ginger (*Alpinia zerumbet*) and the Formosan one (*Hedychium coronarium*).

An account of this garden would not be complete without mentioning all the birds to be seen. There are four different types of humming bird plus the banana quits, the vireos, bullfinches and doves, to mention the more common varieties. There are nineteen different butterflies. Early in the morning there is the possibility of seeing other inhabitants such as agoutis and manicou, and sometimes the crapaud and couess. In addition to the plans for extending the garden, there is also a proposal to create a self-guided garden walk. There is a map already but a more comprehensive one is planned. It will help everyone to enjoy this lovely place even more.

Hotel, restaurant and shop
Telephone (Mrs Anne Jno Baptiste): 448–2287

RIDGEFIELD

This garden with its Victorian overtones belonged to the Dupigny family. After three or four years of comparative neglect it has been taken over by a younger generation of the family, there having been an interregnum on the death of Mr Clem Dupigny. The new owner and carer for the garden is Mrs Johnson and in a very short space of time she has been able to restore the garden almost to its former state. The garden is situated in the hills above Roseau and is reached by the usual winding, climbing Dominican road. The house stands on an eminence in a valley and the garden slopes down on either side of the house, in one direction towards a stream, in the other the valley holds citrus and other fruit orchards. The entrance to the house is down a slope and on either side of the drive are Victorian-type parterres. These parterres are planted with roses and alyssum and other beds contain cannas, lilies and agapanthus. On the lawn on one side there is an azalea which is an unusual sight in Dominica. The soil is acid but one would think the temperature would be too high. On one side of the drive are both pink and red bougainvillea and there are several ixoras plus orange, yellow and red dracaena. There is an old bottle brush tree (*Callistemon citrinus*) with pink begonias planted round it. Further up the sloping lawn is a poinciana tree (*Delonix regia*) and close to it a purple bougainvillea scrambling into and through other trees. There are clumps of yellow day lilies (*Hemerocallis*) around the lawn. Round the side of the house is a big old date tree (*Phoenix dactylifera*) with

Luxuriant growth in the valley.

Allamanda cathartica draping itself through its fronds looking for all the world as if the date had acquired a new type of flower. Below this are more red bougainvilleas. Along the edge of the stream are torch lilies (*Etlingera elatior*) towering up and variegated *Alpinia zerumbet* plus a clump of fishtail palms (*Caryota mitis*). At the back of the house, standing on the lawn, is a very big old mango tree (*Mangifera indica*). It is possibly older than the house. Nearby is an equally big tamarind (*Tamarindus indica*). From the veranda at the back of the house is a lovely view of the sea in the distance and one looks down on coffee and bananas, citrus and sweetsop (*Annona squamosa*), and soursop (*Annona muricata*) all in the orchard in the valley. The orange bird of paradise (*Strelitzia reginae*) has been planted along the retaining wall of the veranda and edging down towards the orchard are yellow croton, more dracaena and double red hibiscus. There is even a pink oleander (*Nerium oleander*) amongst all this. There could not be a bigger contrast between this garden and that of Papillote but that is the fascination.

> Mrs Johnson does welcome visitors but would appreciate notice of a visit.

ST LUCIA

Gardens

DIAMOND BOTANICAL GARDENS
SOUFRIERE, ST LUCIA

In the eighteenth century, the curative powers of natural mineral waters for rheumatism, gout and other ailments were widely recognised and used. Drinking and bathing in the waters at spas like Bath, Buxton and Harrogate in England and Vichy, Evian and Aix-les-Bains in France were highly popular. In the Caribbean, the Bath Hotel and Spring House on the island of Nevis became the principal health resort for the residents of the English colonies of the region. Built as a commercial enterprise by the Huggins family in 1778 at a cost of £40 000, a huge sum in those days, it had a ballroom and rooms for 50 guests. Its patrons included weak or injured soldiers and elderly planters suffering from rheumatism and gout. Henry Nelson Coleridge, nephew of the poet, Samuel Coleridge, complained after a visit in 1825 that the establishment was too big but added that *an invalid with a good servant might take up his quarters here with more comfort than in any other house of public reception in the Caribbean.*

The mineral baths at Soufriere on St Lucia became the principal health resort for the residents of the French islands in the Caribbean (St Lucia was then a French possession). The estate of Soufriere was given to the Devaux

115

family by Louis XIV in 1713. The estate subsequently produced cotton, tobacco, coffee and cocoa. Through the estate runs what are today known as the Diamond Falls, so called on account of the multi-coloured mineral deposits around the falls. They begin as clean, fresh water that runs into sulphur springs in a huge collapsed volcano crater. The water becomes heated to about 180°F and is saturated with minerals before it cascades from the centre of the volcano about 1,800 feet down the mountainside in six falls of varying height. The falls tumble down a hill through mineral-streaked rock walls and jungle-thick ferns into a stream that flows through underground pipes to a series of baths of different temperatures. The water is now at a temperature of about 106°F. One of the geological attractions of the island, the waterfall changes colour, from yellow to black to green to grey, several times a day.

Samples of these waters were sent to Paris for analysis by Baron de Micoud, then Governor of the island. They were found to contain curative properties similar to those of the water at Aix-les-Bains and the baths were constructed in 1784 on the instructions of Louis XVI with the particular intention that they would be used in the cure of wounded or ill French soldiers or sailors fighting in the Caribbean.

Taking a cure at a spa usually involved a stay of some time, drinking just one or two cups of water a day or alternatively taking a similar number of baths a day. The patrons of the resort were left therefore during long

Diamond Falls, St Lucia. (Michael Bourne)

periods of the day with nothing to do. The resort promoters saw it as part of their job to devise entertainments which would fill in the hours while the patrons were waiting for their next drink or next bath. The creation of beautiful gardens and parks in which the customers might take the air was one of the devices used. Spas, both in Europe and in the Caribbean, were famous for their beautiful public gardens. The baths of St Lucia were no exception but were sadly severely damaged by a hurricane in 1780. What remained was levelled during the French Revolution (1789).

The estate is still owned by the interrelated Devaux and Du Boulay families. Before World War II, Andre du Boulay began to restore the baths, using as a foundation the fragments of the originals that remained. Patrick Leigh Fermor enjoyed the simple re-installation during his visit in the 1950s:

The baths were a row of stone troughs in a wooden enclosure in the thick of the woods. Herbert roused an old man from his sleep in a little hut, who stopped up the holes in a trough with plugs of banana leaf. They filled up with warm sulphurous water and we were able to recline in the leafy shade and converse at our leisure, with the craters hissing gently above us.

Mrs Devaux, the wife of the present owner, is in the process of recreating an elegant garden atmosphere for the baths. From the entrance under an umbrella of palms and gigantic tree ferns, a narrow walkway bordered by red ginger lilies, torch lilies and other tropical flowers leads to the baths which are surrounded by well-maintained gardens and a tropical arboretum in addition to the native forest vegetation. Among the interesting trees are the breadnut, a variety of the common breadfruit (*Artocarpus altilis*), the fruit having greenish conical, spine-like projections on its surface, the gri-gri or lady palm (*Rhapis excelsa*) which is distiguished for its hairy, fibrous trunk, and dwarf poinciana, or Pride of Barbados (*Caesalpinia pulcherrima*), possibly a native

Caesalpinia pulcherrima is often used as a hedging plant.

117

of Madagascar but particularly appropriate here as its common name is derived from the Count de Poinci who was once Governor of St Lucia.

An aqueduct carries water to the Great House of the 2000 acre Soufriere estate. The Great House, which is also now open to the public, is surrounded by attractive gardens which have also been developed by Mrs Devaux in recent years. Mrs Devaux and her husband, Robert, who is head of the St Lucia National Trust, are pioneers in the conservation of St Lucia's heritage. The new gardens are focused on an open gazebo set in the middle of an extensive clearing in the natural forest, the open lawns being decorated with colourful island beds. A walk winds around the edge of the clearing and passes through a variety of garden areas: a shade area, a rockery, a lily bank, a wetland area and a pergola, each featuring plants appropriate to their particular area. The ideal of variety within an overall unity of conception and design is thus achieved.

Open daily 8.00 am to 4.00 pm.
Telephone (Walter Zephrin): 450–1520

ST VINCENT

Introduction and history

St Vincent is one of the volcanic islands of the Caribbean. The modern state refers to itself as St Vincent and the Grenadines, and administratively this may be so, but in fact in almost every other way Dominica is its sister island. Like St Vincent, Dominica is volcanic and the history of its Carib peoples tallies with that of St Vincent.

St Vincent is tear-shaped with its great volcano Soufriere still uneasily active at the northern end. Its main town Kingstown is at the southern end. The lushly covered green mountains sweep down to the sea and from the water one can see what appear to be range after range of mountains climbing back towards Soufriere. There are both black and gold beaches. Black sand sounds very glamorous and different but in fact is remarkably uncomfortable to walk on as it retains the heat of the sun like the top of a stove. There is a brooding quality to the island. The valleys are deep, the roads mostly wind along the shore on very steep inclines; the view from the edge of valleys is one of phenomenal growth, the variety is very beautiful. The valley of Mesopotamia (presumably a Biblical allusion) winds between the mountains. There is a rushing river at its bottom and, up the sides, terraced in many places, grow great plantations of bananas and coconuts with occasional small plots of other crops for the farmers' personal use. The east coast of St Vincent is rocky

with long swells pounding in, the west coast is tranquil, sheltered from the prevailing wind. Apart from Kingstown all the settlements are small, some more brightly painted and prosperous than others that have felt the effects of Soufriere's last eruption. Bananas are the main crop and at certain times the roads are full of overloaded, small swaying trucks on their way to the big ships lying in the harbour at Kingstown. Arrowroot is also grown in large quantities. It is of very high quality and has found a new role in modern life – processing computer paper. Spices are produced and much of the usual tropical fruit can be found in the market – mangoes in particular. As long ago as 1596 the tobacco of St Vincent was mentioned as being of good quality but it is not grown today as a commercial crop.

Gardening climate

Like many of the other Caribbean islands formed by volcanic activity, St Vincent has a mountainous core and very limited lowlands around the coasts. It is subject to violent tropical storms and hurricanes, with the highest rainfall occurring between May and July. The highest rainfall is on the windward side. The type of agriculture practised in St Vincent is governed by the rainfall. Bananas have been the biggest crop, and sugar-cane has been tried, but this needs flat or gently undulating land.

The valley known as Mesopotamia with palm trees growing on its steep sides.

Gardening soils

With the steep terrain of much of St Vincent, soil erosion is a problem. In order to keep the soil from being washed away a system of bench terracing has evolved in which the hillside is broken up into a number of steps. The broad banks of earth reduce the speed and amount of water running down the slopes and help to control soil loss and moisture, and therefore fertility. In the island 75% of the land under permanent cultivation is on slopes of over 20°, but the soil is kept covered by growing crops or straw. Manchineel trees are used as soil retainers in the coastal regions, but the tree has poisonous fruits and sap. The soils themselves are latosols, sometimes called laterite, with large amounts of iron, dark and sticky.

Gardening history

The early history of St Vincent is similar to the other islands. It did not seem to have the importance of Dominica because it was not the first landfall. The island was populated by Caribs who were not welcoming to European settlers. In 1635 a ship full of negro slaves was wrecked, they got ashore, settled happily with the Caribs and intermarried. Because of wind and tide, escaping slaves from Barbados were also able to make their way to St Vincent. These two facts subtly altered the ethnic mix of the island and gave rise to what were known as the Black Caribs as opposed to the Yellow Caribs, who were pure-blooded Caribs. The Black Caribs were anti-English from their experiences as slaves in Barbados.

In 1765, in the midst of controversy with the Caribs, the first botanic garden in the western hemisphere was established outside Kingstown, St Vincent. In Britain, knowledge and curiosity about the plants of the world was widespread amongst the well educated. It was realised that plants taken from their original countries could be of use in other lands. Prizes were offered to encourage the ideals of the Society for the Encouragement of Arts, Manufactures and Commerce and land was acquired outside Kingstown for use as a garden to grow experimental plants, acclimatise others and later to encourage diversity of planting amongst the planters. This garden was the first of several to follow in other islands.

Information about St Vincent in the early nineteenth century seems sparse. The few Black Caribs who had escaped expulsion after an uprising were pardoned in 1805 and given 250 acres of land. The botanical garden thrived in its early years but after its devoted curator Alexander Anderson died it went into decline and, amongst other things, some of its plants were transferred to Trinidad to form the nucleus of a garden there. There was a very bad hurricane in 1819 that did enormous damage, particularly to the shipping in the harbour. Because of the wooden houses and the tearing wind, fire spread rapidly through Kingstown.

The abolition of slavery in 1833 had the same traumatic effect in St Vincent as in the other islands. The movement to abolish slavery had started in the late eighteenth century in Britain, particularly endorsed by the non-

Lieutenant Caddy's picture of Fort Charlotte, St Vincent, which was built on one of the hills guarding the harbour of Kingstown.

conformist churches who had a strong presence in St Vincent. The first steps were to try to improve the conditions of slaves but there was great opposition from the planters. The ex-slaves were very anxious to acquire land in order to farm for themselves both for subsistence and cash crops. One positive effect was the diversification of crops. Instead of sugar only, arrowroot was introduced as well as cotton, various spices and bananas. Coffee had been grown on some estates in the previous century. Labour on the estates had become a problem with the abolition of slavery but some ex-slaves were prepared to work in exchange for a house and a piece of land. However disease of crops, poor harvesting methods and inefficient marketing were all problems.

As the century passed the standard of living declined. In the 1880s the British Government became alarmed. A Royal Commission was appointed in 1882 and another in 1896 because the islands of the Caribbean were so in debt. The main recommendations were that crops should be diversifed and more fruit should be grown. Sugar as a profitable crop was in decline because of the competition from sugar beet being grown in Europe. A Department of Agriculture for the West Indies was established in Barbados in 1898. It was to co-ordinate the work of the botanic gardens and stations which were to be set up in different islands. Lecturers and demonstrators would travel from island to island to teach new methods of cultivation and to distribute better varieties of seeds to planters and farmers.

The St Vincent Botanic Garden was all but a wilderness but the same piece of land was used to start what was referred to as the botanic station. This title inferred that the area under cultivation was between three and 30 acres and was reckoned to be of the third grade in the hierarchy of botanic establishments. Its functions were those of an experimental station devoted to the work of maintaining conditions for the propagation and distribution of economic plants. The officer in charge was a well-trained gardener, usually referred to as the curator. Many of the interesting trees of the old garden remained and the revamping of the garden started in 1890 with a speech given to the House of Assembly by the then Governor, Sir Walter Hely-Hutchinson, saying he had been in communication with Kew to request plants and assistance. One of his motives was to improve the cultivation of arrowroot which

had suffered a decline because Bermuda was growing a better quality product.

St Vincent in the twentieth century went through the same political upheavals and alterations as its sister islands. It is now self-governing and independent and the main modern crops are bananas, coconut, spices and arrowroot, with the new crop of flowers.

The redhead calliandra (*Calliandra inaequilatera*) is colloquially known as the powder puff tree because of the shape of its flower heads.

Gardens

❧ THE BOTANIC GARDENS ❧

These gardens were established in 1765 and were the first botanic gardens in the Caribbean. It was realised that a far wider range of plants could probably be grown in the Caribbean than had been tried up to that date. This could contribute considerably to trade. There was also a growing awareness that some of the crops that were being grown resulted in impoverishment of the soil. This applied especially to sugar-cane and cotton. There was a dawning environmental awareness that the clearing of land, particularly of all the trees for crops such as sugar-cane, altered the climate and in particular the rainfall. There was also concern about food supplies. Most food was imported but in times of war and or blockade life became very precarious. There were a large number of slaves and cheap food was needed for them. Added to these concerns was the curiosity which had been engendered by exploration in the Far East, the Pacific and Australia. The Dutch dominated the spice trade during the seventeenth century and had established gardens at the Cape of Good Hope and Mauritius to acclimatise plants before bringing them on to Europe. Other nations now wanted to break that monopoly and with suitable land available in the Caribbean could see the possibility. Sir Joseph Banks, later President of the Royal Society, who had travelled on the *Endeavour* with Captain Cook to the South Seas, was a prime mover in this. In 1754 the Society for the Encouragement of Arts,

Manufactures and Commerce was formed in London. In 1760 the Society issued a list of plants they wished to see experimentally grown *in the American colonies* and offered prizes as an incentive. The list consisted of olives, opium, cinnamon, nutmeg, mace, sarsaparilla, aloe, safflower, indigo, cotton, annatto, vanilla, cloves, pepper, camphor, quinine, various tinctorial plants and ornamental woods amongst others.

The Treaty of Paris of 1763 allotted St Vincent, Grenada, Dominica and Tobago to Britain. The first Governor of the Windward federation of islands was General Robert Melville, a founding member of the Society for the Encouragement of Arts, Manufactures and Commerce. He visited St Vincent on his tour of inspection and met the medical officer for the island, Dr George Young, a keen horticulturist. General Melville saw the opportunity to establish a botanic garden and bought a 20-acre plot of land about a mile outside the capital, Kingstown, and had it cleared. He appointed Dr Young as superintendent. More land was added in 1766. So successful was Dr Young in his endeavours that he was awarded a silver medal and 55 guineas by the Society. The layout of the garden at this time was very similar to what it is today.

The Botanic Gardens are approached up the gently sloping hill from Kingstown. There is a central roadway leading from the entrance (now adorned with wrought iron gates giving the founding date of the gardens) all the way up the garden. Government House can be glimpsed at the top of the garden. Originally the gardens included the Government House land too but in its decline of the nineteenth century this land was taken for the Governor's residence. A river tumbles down a small ravine running through the garden and a circular walk round the edge of the gardens has paths leading away up the hill where large trees are planted. The layout is illustrated in the drawings and paintings done in the eighteenth century. You can still stand on the spot where the paintings were done and look out over the same view.

In 1775 the Society offered a prize for transporting breadfruit (*Artocarpus altilis*) to the West Indies. This offer prompted Bligh's famous expeditions to the South Seas. It was hoped that breadfruit would feed the slave population. At the same time plants were coming in for trial from all over the globe: Asia, North America, Trinidad, Cayenne, Dominica and England. The French were also transporting plants in the hope of growing them in their possessions in the West Indies: Haiti, Martinique and Guadeloupe. During one of the periods of hostilities between France and Britain Lord Rodney captured a French ship which was laden with plants. He distributed the plants to Jamaica and later some of these were sent on to St Vincent. Mango, mangosteen, jak fruit (*Artocarpus heterophyllus*), screw pine (*Pandanus* sp) and women's tongue (*Albizia lebbeck*) were included in that consignment. The French occupation of St Vincent between 1778 and 1782 luckily was not detrimental to the gardens as the French commander General de Bouille was an old friend of Sir Joseph Banks and General Melville.

In 1783 Dr Alexander Anderson arrived as superintendent of the gardens. He was a man in tune with his times. He was an environmentalist as well as being a botanist and gardener. He had an influence far greater than would be

The mulberry is a native of North America and Asia that has adapted well to the Caribbean.

expected of a Director of the St Vincent gardens. He wrote various papers for the Linnean Society, and travelled in South America as well as the so far virtually unexplored parts of St Vincent itself. It was thought for many years that the Soufriere tree, St Vincent's national tree, had been discovered by Anderson on the volcano Soufriere before a later eruption wiped out the flora. However, examination of his notes has proved that he found it in South America from which he also brought back the true black pepper (*Piper nigrum*) and two plants of the nutmeg (*Myristica fragrans*). He made a trip to Guyana in 1791 and in 1798 he wrote a letter to the Society detailing the state of the gardens. He recorded that Dr Young had introduced cinnamon, which was already found in 'Martinico' and was the same as that found in Ceylon, thirty years before, and from three small trees in 1785 one hundred trees had been grown, all producing seed. Anderson also recorded that clove had been received at the same time. In 1798 Anderson got a Silver Medal from The Society of Arts for his work at the gardens and a house was built in it for him, which deteriorated rapidly from the heavy rainfall and the termites. In 1798 he made a comprehensive list of the plants growing in the gardens. The breadfruit, about which so much has been written and recorded, arrived in 1793 after the completion of Bligh's second voyage which was successful from every point of view, the plants arriving in very good condition. Five hundred and thirty plants were left in St Vincent and the rest went on to Jamaica and to Kew Gardens. Anderson worked very hard over the breadfruit and was very proud of his success. The first fruit started to form only a year after their arrival. A slip of those original trees still grows in the gardens, now a large tree itself.

In 1803 another ten acres were added to the gardens. The original land had been too steep for seedlings and the soil was often washed away. There is a rather sad 1806 letter from Anderson recounting how the planters of the island would not give land for the growing of the breadfruit trees, claiming as their excuse that the negroes did not like it which Anderson said was not true. He complained bitterly of the planters' improvidence and chopping down trees and said the war was affecting further supplies of plants for the gardens. In 1811 Alexander Anderson died, a great loss to the botanical world. Interest in botanic gardens had waned by this time because the British royal family no longer expressed the keen interest they had before.

William Lochead was appointed to succeed Alexander Anderson but he died three years later and was succeeded by George Caley, a Kew trained man who was a protégé of Sir Joseph Banks. He was not accepted socially and was involved frequently in quarrels with the neighbouring planters and the general public. When he discovered plants were being stolen from the gardens by Sunday visitors, he shut the gardens. He returned to England in 1823 after resigning. This offered the local government the chance it had been looking for; the expense of the gardens had become burdensome. A new botanical garden had been started in Trinidad, so as many plants as possible were sent to it. The task in St Vincent was merely to harvest the large crops of nutmegs, cloves and other produce and to keep the garden tidy. In 1828 a three-acre portion was set aside for the new Government House which was built on the site of the original superintendent's house.

In 1830 it was commented *that the only improvement that had taken place was the destruction of the manager's house and the erection by the colony of a very pretty cottage instead. The garden was no longer in a state of cultivation though it still*

The nursery at the Botanic Gardens – note the lettuce growing on the roof of the shelter.

contains many rare and valuable treasures ... the clove, the nutmeg and the cinnamon. It is said horses are allowed to wander in the garden grazing and trampling down the shrubs and trees. The colony has entirely given up the place.

By 1861, *the famed botanic garden twenty years ago the pride of St Vincent and celebrated throughout the West Indies can not now even be distinguished.*

Luckily this was not the end of the Botanic Gardens. In the late 1880s alarm was once more being felt about the state of the West Indian islands and their economies. Part of the solution was the setting up of a network of botanic gardens and stations. The Trinidad garden had been continuing its work since its establishment in 1819, and Barbados had had its own establishment. Jamaica had had various gardens and at this time was distributing seed to other islands. By 1890 the Governor of St Vincent, Sir Walter Hely Hutchinson, gave a speech announcing he was in communication with Kew and he hoped to encourage the growing of new commercial plants and the distribution of seeds and plants. Dr Daniel Morris, who was an assistant director of Kew and had previously worked in Jamaica, made a trip through the West Indies to facilitate the establishment of a West Indian Commission to set up the network of necessary gardens and botanic stations. Funding was organised and, luckily for St Vincent, she was eligible for imperial funds. The new botanic gardens rose on the site of the old. Thirteen acres were first cleared in May 1890 and Mr H Powell was appointed curator. A visitor commented: *since May 1890 Powell has converted the jungle into a pretty botanic garden ... a nice little ornamental house is being built nearer his work.*

One of the most useful tasks for the new curators and head gardeners was to make a collection for a herbarium. Powell, with the help of two other visiting Englishmen, was able to make one of St Vincent flora. It is still regarded as a valuable early record and is now in Kew. By 1897 the gardens had progressed so well under the care of Powell that an impressive number of plants were for sale. Amongst others, *twenty-three different fruits and economic plants, five kinds of vines, five hundred specimens of* Eichhornia crassipes, *the water hyacinth, two kinds of orchids, seven kinds of ferns and fourteen kinds of roses.* It is possible the water hyacinths we see today in a neglected pond are the descendants of these.

There was a devastating hurricane in 1898 but many plants were replaced by a good friend living in Dominica who had benefited from the St Vincent garden. The following comment on a subsequent volcanic eruption was published in the *Gardenener's Chronicle* of May 24th 1902: *The island of St Vincent is, at present, the scene of a terrible tragedy, the equal of which is not in the memory of man. But this far off island is not unaccustomed to the terrible for in 1898 there happened a hurricane which committed such great havoc, that recovery was not completed on the occurrence of the present disturbance. The botanic station had proved a great success in the distribution of seeds to small proprietors ... In a matter of hours many of the best estates were ruined and many hundreds of trees sacrificed, the earth blasted by heavy showers of ashes and dust.* In the December 13th, 1902 edition: *Another eruption in October, the curator of the Botanic Gardens reports further serious damage.* Presumably it was Soufriere erupting, something that even today has to be taken into account as a possibility in St Vincent.

The Doric temple, fountain and lily pool.

Mr Powell was transferred to East Africa in 1904 in the way of the then Colonial Service and was followed by William Sands. This was probably the high point for the gardens. Although responsible for many other schemes on the island such as an agricultural school, a stock farm, a land settlement scheme and the government cotton ginnery he still made time to consider the gardens. He wanted to make them more accessible to visitors and for this purpose roads were levelled and widened and one could drive round without even leaving one's carriage. In 1912–13 the Doric temple was built in the middle of the gardens, complete with lily pool and a drinking fountain in the shape of the inverted bell of the yellow allamanda flower. Seats were provided to enable visitors to enjoy the view. Sands also started the custom of any important visitors planting a tree in memory of their visit. A young mahogany tree was planted by Princess Marie Louise of Schleswig-Holstein.

The true purpose of the gardens was not forgotten and the original experiments in growing the cotton that proved to be the pride of St Vincent because of its wonderful soft quality, were conducted here. Arrowroot (*Maranta arundinacea*), sugar-cane (*Saccharum officinarum*) and cocoa (*Theobroma cacao*) were also grown experimentally here. A co-operative for the growing of arrowroot was formed and this became a major export crop to the world markets – again because of its excellent quality.

In 1944 the experimental work was transferred to Camden Park and the Botanical Garden was left as an ornamental garden. Unfortunately the labelling is not good. There are still a lot of large trees. At one time there were many mahoganies but wasps decimated them through destroying the seed. The large trees mostly stand round the edges of the gardens and up the steep slope above the old curator's house. There is a pink poui (*Tabebuia pentaphylla*), a *Jacaranda acutifolia*, and a big *Cassia fistula* whose beans have a medicinal use as an emetic. There is a huge red mahoe which is a native of the north of St Vincent and the blue mahoe (*Hibiscus elatus*) which is a native of Jamaica. Not far away is the strange but handsome cannonball tree (*Couroupita guianensis*) with its leaves emerging from the top half of the tree and the flowers which are heavily scented straight from the trunk. There is

the Honduras mahogany (*Swietenia macrophylla*) as well as *S. mahogani*.

Another group consists of the rubber tree from Brazil, a Central American rubber and a Lagos silk rubber. Nearby is an ackee tree (*Blighia sapida*) now associated with Jamaica as its national fruit but originally from Africa. Nearby is the eye-catching traveller's palm (*Ravenala madagascariensis*), so called because of the cache of water to be found at the base of each leaf. (This tree grows prolifically in the wild in Mauritius.) Here it soars to a great height above the gardens. Near it are cinnamon trees (descendants presumably of the original imports), the paradise nut and the brazil nut which are of the same family as the cannonball tree.

There is still a collection of palms in the gardens such as sealing wax palms (*Cyrtostachys renda*) with their brilliant red trunks which catch the eye, majestic royal palms (*Roystonea*) and the rattan palms (*Calamus*). The trumpet tree (*Cecropia peltata*) also features – a tree of rapid growth from which canoes are made. Not far away is the great spire of a Norfolk Island pine (*Araucaria excelsa*), originally from the tiny island in the Pacific. There is also a Trinidad cedar which provides a red wood which is good for furniture. You will come upon the Soufriere tree here which although it flowers does not set seed. The big eucalyptus was planted in 1904. The buttercup tree (*Cochlospermum vitifolium*), although seen throughout the Caribbean, is not that common and is a spectacular sight when in flower because its leaves are not out at the same time as the flowers. There is a frangipani (*Plumeria*) collection with all its different colours. There is another collection of aromatic

plants, which includes the plant for chaulmoogra oil which cures leprosy. On the way out of the gardens, on the walk down hill, there are two huge *Jacaranda acutifolia*, known locally as fern trees, their trunks covered with the yellow cat's claw vine (*Macfadyena unguisaeti*). The scent of a nearby ylangylang (*Cananga odorata*) follows one. This garden is a lovely place, tranquil and memorable. It is maintained but one could but wish that the labelling was better and more funding was available to care for and develop a place that is unique.

The gardens are owned by the National Trust.
The gardens are open from 10.00 am to 6.00 pm.
The office is open from 10.00 am to 4.00 pm.
Telephone: 457–1003

An old jacaranda tree with a covering of cat's claw vine.

❧ MONTREAL GARDENS 🌿

High up in the foothills of the mountains at the head of the Mesopotamia valley, beyond the village of the same name and Richmond Park, lies a dream garden. Once much loved and well-established, it is now very overgrown but for a plantsman and gardener it is still a place of enchantment. It is like *The Secret Garden*. The road up to it is very twisting and one is beginning to feel one can't get any higher into the mountains without getting out of the car and climbing, when one comes upon a high bank covered with flowers and a grassy entrance. Up the grassy drive between bending oleanders one comes upon a ruined wooden house standing in a clearing. On walking round to the front of the house one discovers a garden consisting of rows, which were once raised beds, of a mixture of anthuriums, dracaena, cannas and *Heliconia psittacorum*. The beds were originally made with a base of coconut shell but all has melded into a colourful mass. Beyond this a lookout has been arranged for the visitor to admire the amazing view of the east shore many thousands of feet below and the towering mountains behind. Behind this there are winding paths that lead down the hill past a small lily pool which was once also the site of a restaurant. Above the path large nutmeg trees (*Myristica fragrans*) shower down their fruit, and there is a very large *Bauhinia purpurea* tree and several sword trees (*Erythrina coralladendrum*) as well as African tulip trees (*Spathodea campanulata*). To the right of the path is a citrus orchard, the trees covered not only in fruit but furry bromeliads. Down again

Heliconia growing wild in Montreal Gardens.

goes the path across tree roots till it reaches the river. By the river the path goes both ways but along here great torch lilies (*Etlingera elatior*) arch over your head. Another tiny wooden cottage rests on a platform over the river and there are several lacy tree ferns (*Cyathea*). It is a place of silence except for birds calling and the rustle of leaves. On

131

the opposite bank of the river is a wood of *Casuarina equisetifolia* trees. The path curves round again through the orchard to meet the drive by the house. It is a garden once much loved and then neglected for a variety of reasons. It is worked on by one lone gardener who loves it, and there is a plan by the new owner to restore it, rebuild the houses and make a restaurant once again.

> Gardens open 10.00 am to 4.00 pm Monday through Friday.
> Closed Saturday and Sunday
> Admission fee EC$10.00.
> Telephone (Timothy Vaughan, owner or Mr Jackson): 458–5452

 MOUNT WILLIAM

Mount William is an old estate in the foothills of the mountains facing the east coast with La Soufriere in the background. To reach it you take the road up the east side of the island (on the map it is about half-way up, south of Georgetown and the turning to the west is at the village of Byera). On some of the maps it is marked as 'Cocoa Factory' on the road up to the Byera Valley. It was this land with access to the eastern shore that was regarded as such valuable land for the original sugar plantations.

The house stands on a knoll above valleys on either side of it. The road passes on one side in the valley, a river flows down the other valley. This plenteous supply of water from the mountains is a wonderful resource and the owners have built water tanks to hold water in reserve. The soil is acid and slightly sandy but the estate is moderately sheltered from the strong sea winds of the eastern shore, except in the event of a hurricane. The land is now used as a mixed farm, as it was in the past, growing sugarcane, cocoa, coconuts and tobacco. A scheme has recently been started by the owners to grow bananas on a sharecropper basis. The slopes of the valley are planted with areas of bananas; the farmworkers and 'hands' plant and share in the results of the crop. A new mango orchard has recently been planted.

The newest venture for the estate has been started by Mrs Denise Punnett, who has a plant nursery. She does all the propagating herself and her crowded nursery is on the same ridge as the house, under the shade of some of the original trees of the estate like a big mango (*Mangifera indica*) and a lime tree (*Citrus aurantifolia*). She is growing plants with the new gardener and householder in mind. It is a new idea in St Vincent to have a plant nursery – previously people acquired plants only from friends. She is supplying the gardens of Mustique so she is concentrating on seaside planting, that is salt- and wind-tolerant plants, and is now turning her talents towards landscaping. She has already completed some gardens on St Vincent and has had some commissions on Mustique too.

In the area near the house there are the smaller plants in pots: kalanchoe, asparagus fern (*Asparagus sprengeri*) and a big leafed fern (*Polypodium aureum*) which can be used as ground cover. There are large vanda plants which are trained up supports, the ever popular croton, the variegated

The plant nursery at Mount William.

dieffenbachia and many pots of bougainvillea. There are hanging baskets for verandas and patios filled with pelargoniums and other trailing plants. There is also a monstera and a large staghorn fern. Philodendrons and small mussaendas are here as well as heliconias. She also has plants of a miniature oleander (*Nerium oleander*) which would be useful for confined areas, *Allamanda cathartica* and small scarlet cordias (*Cordia sebestena*). Ixoras are a popular and easily propagated and grown plant. Of course Mrs Punnett has many different coloured hibiscus, the equally popular *Begonia semperflorens* and the more unusual jade vine (*Strongylodon macrobotrys*) growing up one of the shade trees.

Down the drive towards the road one comes upon the large plant nursery under shading made from black netting. Here there are both trees and shrubs, some in quite large quantities because, as Mrs Punnett says, when someone comes in and asks for 24 palms for a driveway, that depletes her stock rapidly. She has a good selection: the golden palm (*Chrysalidocarpus lutescens*), the fan palm (*Pritchardia pacifica*), *Latania borbonica* and *Coccothrinax argentea*. No nursery would be complete without a selection of heliconias and torch ginger (*Etlingera elatior*), all of which she has. She is also growing the traveller's palm (*Ravenala madagascariensis*), which makes a very handsome specimen plant, and a lot of saman trees which are quick growing and so ideal for a new garden and easily propagated. There are young mahoganies and ficus (the latter are also quick growing). Of the large shrubs she has mussaenda, pigeon berry, big bougainvilleas and poinsettias which form a good size shrub in the climate of St Vincent.

The tree nursery at Mount William.

The last call in this interesting property is the orchid nursery. Down in the valley not far from the river is a large shade house (made from black netting again) of 5000 square feet. This is designed for growing orchids and in here are 20 000 phalaenopsis plants. They are grown on raised beds of coconut shell. It is not as big a venture as Victor Hadley's on Union Estate nearby, but it is still very impressive. The idea of growing orchids commercially, and for both local trade and export, is a comparatively new one for St Vincent.

Mrs Punnett is very pleased to see visitors but as she is both hard working and busy she hopes they will have a serious interest in plants.
Telephone: 458–6210

❧ UNION ESTATE (HADLEY BLOOMS) ✿

Mr Victor Hadley's estate, Union, lies off the east shore road, between the villages of North and South Union. Marked on the maps with the words 'Copra Factory' it lies at a height of 1000 feet. His family have farmed in St Vincent for the last two hundred years, but this estate is the last of three originally owned by the family. The house stands up a long drive on a hill above the sea. The large plant farm is in a deep valley below, where it can be seen from the house. There are several very large shade sheds. Ten acres are under cultivation altogether, one and

Anthuriums in the shade shed.

a half acres of these planted with orchids, the rest with anthuriums.

The technical difficulties of growing such exotic flowers are incredible. Disease is a very real danger. It can be imported on the bulbs themselves or be brought in on shoes or tyres. For this reason visitors cannot go into the sheds, but a very good view can be had from outside. Anthuriums are grown on raised beds of coconut shell. In spite of the beauty of the present blooms, Mr Hadley says he does not consider coconut shell to be the best medium and he is experimenting both with the shape of the beds (presently a wide U) which is to be converted to a deep V, and a different medium consisting of volcanic soil mixture which is readily available locally from La Soufriere. Achieving the right pH level is difficult. As with so many plants 5.5 is ideal, but going down to 3 is acceptable. However the acid water upsets this and the feeding must be checked carefully as coconut shell itself, being acidic, alters the level. There is a plentiful supply of water from a river running through the nursery – so plentiful at times that the bridge across it is submerged. This water is stored in tanks. Coconut shell is also very prone to harbouring fungus which is another reason for trying to find another growing medium. The plants are inspected every day; the large area is sub-divided and the sub-divisions are the individual responsibility of one of the work force. Root rot can be a problem and heavy rain, which comes through the netting, does do damage. Every day the plants have exactly ninety seconds of fertiliser applied consistently through a sophisticated and computerised watering system. Fungicide is also sprayed from the system.

One of the spectacular blooms grown on Union Estate. This one is *Anthurium andraeanum* var.

The area around the sheds has to be kept clean because weeds are inclined to bring whitefly; luckily whitefly do not like anthuriums. Several colours of anthurium are grown. There are pure white ones, pink and green (called obaki), peach and at least two different reds with the dark red ones being the strongest plants. There are two acres of red anthuriums alone. There is a heart-shaped variety which, though lovely, is particularly prone to fungus. The demand for the different colours is seasonal, with dark red for winter and Christmas, white and peach for summer and weddings. The actual colour of the flowers is brighter in the summer. The plants do live for a long time but in the first two to six years they produce 100 per cent; after a time

Across the stream and up the hill are one and a half acres of shade sheds in which are grown dendrobium orchids. The climate is a bit damp for them ideally but nevertheless they produce perfect blooms. It takes two years for a plant to grow to the correct size for full flowering. The white flowered plants are better producers although there are several rows of the pink. Six thousand sprays a week are cut and sent for export, 800 a week are sold locally for the cut flower trade. In a shed further again up the hill heliconia and ginger plants are also being grown as part of a new expansion and there are many rows of phalaenopsis orchids. From these tissue cultures are being produced, potted up and exported to Europe. Plans for the future include landscaping the area to make a tropical garden as well as ensuring visitors will be able to walk on paths round the outside of some of the plant houses.

A telephone call before visiting would be appreciated. Telephone: 458–6528

The beautiful blooms of phalaenopsis which are also grown for export.

the rate drops merely to 50 per cent. They are cut all the year and 400 boxes a week are exported, packed in shredded newspaper which has been recycled and is clean. It is dampened to protect the flowers which are graded and measured in the cutting house. The cartons are cut to the required size and are sent to the United States, Canada and Europe for the cut flower trade.

 GRENADA

Gardens

❧ BAY GARDENS ☙
MORNE DELICE, GRENADA

Bay Gardens occupy the site of an old sugar mill which is located north-east of the island's capital, St George's. Their general layout does not conform to any formal style, rather it is arranged as an artfully-contrived but natural-looking woodland grove containing many interesting and exotic trees, shrubs, annuals, perennials, bulbs, orchids, climbing and aquatic plants from many parts of the tropical world. The three-acre steeply-sloping site is traversed by a labyrinth of narrow paths which open occasionally to reveal a spreading lawn or a pond or pool. The paths are covered with nutmeg shells. The husks of nutmegs, which remain after processing, are used in gardens throughout the island as a mulch or as a free-draining path material which is ideal for coping with water run-off after a tropical storm.

A focal point amid the array of over 3000 different taxa which have been planted is the lawn around which the collection of palms and other associated trees grow. Most exciting among them is the group of trees which features

Water collects in the leaf stems of this palm – hence its name of traveller's palm (*Ravenala madagascariensis*).

138

Bay Gardens, Grenada (Helen Gasneal)

the screw pine (*Pandanus baptisii*) and its variegated form (*Pandanus sanderi*) as well as the traveller's tree (*Ravenala madagascariensis*). In terms of colour and form these are among the most memorable of tropical trees. The screw pines, native to Polynesia and India, are noteworthy on account of their long leaves which arise in a spiral forma-

tion at the ends of the branches. The spreading limbs of mature specimens are propped by clusters of above-ground stilt-roots which are developed by the tree specifically for that purpose. *Pandanus sanderi* makes a vivid part of a garden picture on account of its leaves which are longitudinally-striped cream and green. The traveller's tree, a native of Madagascar, is curious in that its leaves grow mainly in one vertical plane. Thus mature specimens look like gigantic green fans. Botanically, it is a member of the large banana family, its flower, leaves and fruit being similar to its related genus, the *Strelitzia* or bird of paradise family. Its common name is derived from the fact that its hollow leaf stalks form water receptacles at their base and so can always be used as a source of refreshment. The traveller's tree enjoys the high rainfall in Grenada's hills.

The garden also features many tropical American trees and shrubs, among them many yellow-flowered shrubs such as the candlebush (*Cassia alata*) with its delicate, pinnately-compound foliage and its numerous, erect flower-spikes, and the buttercup tree (*Cochlospermum vitifolium*) with its flowers like single roses or great buttercups which appear on the bare branches after its big, palmate leaves have fallen. The garden is fully and richly planted so that under all of the trees and shrubs is an array of smaller sub-shrubs and other plants. Decorative foliage plants abound: the fire dragon (*Acalypha wilkesiana*) with its embossed, red or bronze foliage which is sometimes margined with white, the more common poinsettias, (*Euphorbia pulcherrima*) and sinister-looking crotons (*Codiaeum* spp). Also much planted are the banana family members, the heliconias, particularly

Heliconia wagneriana, with its tall paddle-shaped leaves and its bi-colour bracts.

The garden ponds are stocked with tropical fish species. One of them is in the form of a turtle aquarium. All of the ponds are extensively planted with marginal and aquatic plants. One of them sports the beautiful water lettuce (*Pistia* spp). The pleated lime-green leaves of these floating plants have a velvety surface that catches and holds raindrops which sparkle in the sunlight after the garden's frequent tropical showers. Areas devoted to orchids, bromeliads and to the demonstration of the island's commercial crops complete the attractions of this garden.

Ornamental plants from many parts of the tropical world have been brought together in the Bay Gardens and are grown in such a natural way that the impression is given of a tropical Eden.

Open daily 7.00 am to 6.00 pm.
Telephone: 440–5338

TOWER HOUSE
ST PAUL'S, GRENADA

Tower House is located in an area of wooded hills behind the island's capital, St George's. In a prominent position, it enjoys distant prospects over the countryside to the sea. The late Victorian/Edwardian villa is constructed in a variety of materials: red brick, grey brick, random-rubble

Tower House (Helen Gasneal)

140

and cut-stone. It is also designed in a variety of architectural styles: High Victorian and Queen Anne Revival with a veranda in a trabeated Indian style. Variety was an effect deliberately sought by architects and their patrons at that time.

Variety is also a keynote of the gardens. The variety of level around the house, for example, has given to the architect the opportunity to design a system of broad terraces and balustraded flights of steps which give a strong underlying framework to the garden on two sides of the house. The framework is softened, however, by the tall trees and shrubs which overhang its geometric lines: angel's trumpet (*Datura rosea*) with its pendant trumpet-like flowers exuding their heavy scent across the terraces in the evening, flame tree (*Delonix regia*) with its scarlet flowers and lacy foliage and the rare, straggling rubber vine (*Cryptostegia grandiflora*).

The architectural formality of this part of the garden leads into a stone-paved walk between twin shrub borders planted to look a little like the twin herbaceous borders which are such a common feature of English gardens. The most striking of the border shrubs are the new bi-colour and tri-colour horticultural varieties of hibiscus which have been imported into Grenada by the pioneering nurseryman, John Criswick, of St Rose's. In the Tower House borders, only varieties with flowers in the soft, pastel colours, rather than the harsher red colours, are used. It is a sensible idea to group the hibiscus together in a single border where they can enjoy the sun and free soil drainage and where they can be watered conveniently. They are also ideal plants for a border in that they can, indeed, benefit

from being pruned regularly to keep them to a predetermined shape and size. Growing in the shade of the hibiscus are the pink forms of the red ginger lilies like *Alpinia purpurata* 'Pink Princess' which were developed in the 1970s and the compact forms of the lobster claw (*Heliconia acuminata*). Also seen are small clerodendrons in variety. They can, like the hibiscus, be pruned hard so they do not outgrow their border location. An elegant rarity in the border is the rose grape (*Medinilla magnifica*), a small square-stemmed shrub with leathery, prominently-veined leaves and pale pink bracts concealing numerous tiny, rose-pink flowers.

Behind the house is an extensive area of level lawn which was only created with great difficulty and expense on this steeply-sloping site. Its smooth evergreen surface provides a calm visual foil for the complex architecture of the house, and a level ground for lawn games like tennis, croquet and bowls as well as for garden furniture. A brass band was a common entertainment at elegant colonial garden parties of the Edwardian age. On the lawn opposite the house is a large *nymphaeum* or recessed niche – constructed unexpectedly with mass concrete – which assumed the role of an acoustic bandshell during garden parties and concerts. It might have appeared to be an uncompromisingly stark 'modern' structure had it not been enriched with a monumental flight of steps and swathed with masses of brightly-coloured bougainvillea.

The formal lawn gradually becomes more natural in shape and more undulating in level as it recedes away from the house at an oblique angle. The character of the planting likewise becomes more informal. Taller trees and

141

shrub-groups in an apparently random arrangement decorate the lawn. The tall pale-grey trunks of Caribbean cabbage palms (*Roystonea oleracea*) lift their heads of long, pinnate leaves to the tropical sky. They punctuate a series of shrub borders laid out in curving perspective so as to lead the eye gradually into the shadows of the woodland behind. Most interesting of the borders is that devoted exclusively to plants with variegated foliage.

Variegated foliage is a matter of some controversy among gardeners – some admire and are stimulated by the striking visual effects which can be created with it, others decry its viral cause and regard the colour effects as too 'loud' amid the ordered calm of a garden. There is no doubt that if variegated shrubs are dotted about the garden they can lead to a restless, unsettled visual effect. However, grouping them together as a feature, in one part of the garden only, as has been done at Tower House, offers an interesting resolution of the dilemma. (This is also a practical solution – since they all depend for their effect on abundant foliage, they all share the need for a high-nitrogen fertiliser.) The border is dominated by a cluster of the variegated coral tree (*Erythrina variegata*), its green leaves boasting prominent yellow venation against which its flame-red flowers compete for attention. They are planted with many variegated horticultural varieties of croton (*Codiaeum variegatum*). These varieties are, of course, distinguished not only by their many different foliage colours – green, yellow, red and purple and many combinations thereof – but also by their many different leaf shapes – oval, undulate, toothed, fringed, narrow-leaved, broad-leaved and oak-leaved. In addition, the variegated colour can show on the leaf in different ways, as spots, blotches, stripes, edges or margins, for example. Crotons are useful border plants in that they will benefit from hard pruning which will keep each shrub to its required size in the border. Their cultivation also requires a rich soil, a high-nitrogen fertiliser, full sun and regular watering so it is sensible from a practical gardening point of view to keep them together in the same border.

The focal point of this part of the garden is a rustic summerhouse and pergola engulfed by a magnificent specimen of the jade vine (*Strongylodon macrobotrys*) which enjoys the rich soil, humidity and heat in this garden. The jade vine is best appreciated if seen growing from a high pergola because then its three feet long hanging racemes, composed of multiple flowers each in the shape of a bird's beak, and of a blue-green colour unique in the vegetable kingdom, can be seen from below.

Tower House is at the centre of a working plantation so the visitor to the garden can enjoy in season the sight of trays of drying cloves and cocoa beans behind the service areas of the house. Since its inception, the garden has been known as one of the best examples in the Caribbean of traditional architecture and design. Now this is complimented with a variety of well-chosen planting to give a richly-colourful effect in all seasons.

Open occasionally to horticultural groups by previous arrangement.

A century plant. (Chris Huxley)

Gazetteer of other gardens in the Windward Islands

✕ BOTANIC GARDENS ⚘
ST GEORGE'S, GRENADA

Founded as a botanical station in 1887 through which new economic and useful plants might be introduced from abroad to Grenada, it now contains a variety of Grenadian plants appropriately labelled and a small adjoining zoo of tropical birds and animals.

✕ CRISWICK NURSERY GARDEN ⚘
ST ROSE, GRENADA

One of the best ornamental plant nurseries in the Caribbean, its owner, John Criswick, has introduced many new plants from abroad to grace Caribbean gardens.

✕ TROPICA GARDENS ⚘
ST LUCIA

A family-owned three-acre garden which has been developed since 1978 with a naturalistic design. Conceived in 1978 and opened to the public in 1994, this is a wild-looking

A red cotton tree (Bombax ceiba).

yet organised garden containing over 1000 plant species and varieties.

Open every day 8.00 am to 4.00 pm by appointment.
Telephone (John de Veer): 452–0661.

⚘ UNION AGRICULTURAL STATION ⚘ MEDICINAL GARDEN
ST LUCIA

The site of the St Lucia Forestry Department headquarters contains a small garden featuring native Caribbean plants which are used in herbal medicines. There is also an interpretive centre, a small zoo featuring the endangered St Lucia parrot and a nature trail running through stands of Caribbean pine (*Pinus caribaea*), latania fan palm (*Latania loddigesii*) and bay rum (*Pimenta racemosa*).

Open daily 8.00 am to 4.00 pm.
Telephone (Mrs Norville): 450–2642

SIX

BARBADOS

Introduction and history

When the Spaniards first landed on Barbados they found the island occupied by the Arawaks. They did not stay long, moving off elsewhere. The Portuguese visited also but did not want to possess the island. However, they left a number of pigs to run wild on the island with the thought that on a future occasion the pigs might provide a useful larder.

Barbados was founded on the 'proprietor' system which meant that the island in question was claimed for England but all founding expenses of the Colony were funded by either an individual or a group of men who formed themselves into a Company. Often the Crown, the King, simply did not have the necessary funds available and was interested only in the tax revenue provided. The Courteen Brothers' company already had interests in Brazil and Guyana and in 1625 they sent out John Powell to claim

The white form of the petrea is just as beautiful as the blue.

Barbados for England. In 1627 Henry Powell (brother to John) arrived in Barbados with 80 men and built a settlement at Holetown, then named Jamestown. As the island is east of the other islands and therefore to windward it was considered protected to some extent from attack. It was uninhabited at this time and although there are no mountains the soil, rich and black, supported forests of dyewood. The forests were so thick the settlers had difficulty exploring the island and getting about or finding anything to eat. The idea was to harvest this valuable timber for sale and plant tobacco. Because the settlers knew nothing of tropical agriculture, a message was sent to Essequibo/Guyana and the Governor sent seeds and Arawaks to show the settlers how to cultivate them. The seeds they brought with them were yams, cassava, maize, plantains, bananas, pineapples, oranges, lemons and limes. Tobacco, cotton and indigo were all planted as cash crops.

Gardening climate

Barbados is a much flatter island than, for example, Dominica, and has a comparatively low rainfall. The climate is a moderate tropical one, with two seasons: dry from December to May, wet from June to November. There is more rain on the hilly central area (about 90 inches per annum). The average for the coastal area is 40 inches. The average temperature in February is 24°C rising to 28°C in September. The island lies on its own to the east of the rest of the Caribbean islands and is in the path of the prevailing north-east trade winds. The land falls in a series of terraces from the hilly backbone to the west and declines more sharply in the east and south. Barbados is almost encircled by coral reefs and is in the hurricane zone.

Gardening soils

Barbados is geologically composed of coral accumulation on sedimentary rocks. It has a fertile, loamy soil with free drainage. Plants of all kinds can be grown over most of the island. There is little surface water, but subterranean water, stored in limestone beds, supports a few natural springs.

Gardening history

The early history of the settlement was not happy, dogged by arguments over the proprietorship. The population grew rapidly. From the 80 who landed in 1627, it became 1600 in 1629, 4000 in 1631 and 30 000 in 1639. This rapid expansion was partly responsible for what was known as 'the starving time'. A lot of these extra people were indentured servants, contracted for a set number of years to an employer in exchange for clothes, food and lodging and some little money, hoping that eventually they would be able to acquire land for themselves in order to farm. There was friction between the planters and the servants because the proprietor, Lord Carlisle was demanding the planters pay tax and as a result the servants were being made to work very hard and often treated with cruelty. Tobacco was the crop that produced tax money and subsistence crops were a low priority. Cassava and maize were the subsistence crops, tobacco and cotton were the exported crops with ginger and indigo making a smaller contribution. There were a few large plantations with indentured servants but most farms were small plots of four hectares worked by the owner and maybe one extra man. Eventually the authorities became so worried by the lack of food crops they ordered the area of tobacco to be reduced and more food grown. Trade had been better in Barbados than St Kitts because of Dutch ships calling to buy salt meat and other food. However this had to be banned because of 'the starving time'.

Some visitors to Barbados at this time were not very impressed with what they saw. There was a great deal of 'slash and burn' agriculture; areas cleared of all their trees, cultivated for a short time and then the cultivation was moved on. The houses were poorly built, the roads bad and, although the House of Assembly had been established in 1639, there was friction amongst the settlers.

The cultivation of sugar in the West Indies was to have far-reaching effects. Tobacco prices had dropped because the quality of Virginia tobacco was much better than that being produced in all the islands. With the exploration

Planting sugar-cane. (Chris Huxley)

and colonisation of the Far East and India coffee and tea became popular drinks and sugar was needed as a sweetener.

Sugar estates were about 60 hectares, sometimes bigger, formed by partnerships but this was the result of combining smaller holdings. These new estates had to be self-supporting so half the land was used for sugar. There was pasture for cattle, arable land for corn, cassava, vegetables and fruit and there had to be woodland for the fuel needed for the sugar mills. Barbados did not have much waste land – unlike St Kitts – and this, together with soil exhaustion (which became a problem) drove up the price of land. The population changed considerably with far fewer white people and many more black ones. Barbados was the island most dramatically affected by the change to sugar cultivation between 1640–50.

About this time Richard Ligon visited Barbados and left a wonderful account of the island at that time. His book was published in 1657. He described in great detail the trees to be found, in particular the palmetto royal (our royal palm – *Roystonea* sp.), calabash (*Crescentia cujete*), allspice which he calls 'Bay' and 'Anchovie Pear' (our avocado – *Persea americana*), guava (*Psidium guajava*) and custard apple (*Annona reticulata*). He also gives detailed descriptions of the birds and animals and 'pismires' or ants. He was fascinated by the processing of sugar and there are drawings of the machinery. He also describe what

Villa Nova, Barbados. (Chris Huxley)

it was necessary to import from England and the expenses of dressing slaves and 'Christian servants'.

During the next hundred years the Caribbean was swept by war, islands being captured and re-captured, changing hands with great frequency, but Barbados remained immune (in the sense she remained British throughout) and was the second most profitable sugar island. The American War of Independence added to the problem because trade routes were cut and Barbados was not producing her own food. The slaves were particularly hard hit and there was famine and near starvation.

The emancipation of the slaves had a dramatic effect on Barbados as it did on all the islands. As Barbados land was mostly taken up with sugar plantations there was very little spare land left for the freed slaves to acquire to farm on their own account. The result was that they returned to work on the plantations but this time for wages. The slaves had always had very small parcels of land on which they had grown provisions and these they were able to keep.

The Royal Commissions of 1882 and 1896 were set up because of the anxiety felt by the British Government about the financial state of the West Indian islands. Their first recommendations were that there should be an increase in the diversity of crops grown, particularly of fruit because the sugar industry was so obviously in decline. They suggested that only Antigua, Barbados and St Kitts should retain sugar as a main crop. Their next suggestion was that a network of botanical gardens and stations should be established throughout the islands in order to grow new plants and provide seeds for the planters and that there should be teaching establishments for the benefit of the local youths. Jamaica was already doing some of this work of distribution. In the *Kew Bulletin* of 1887 this scheme is detailed and figures of exports of fruits from the islands is given. In 1888 the *Kew Bulletin* gave a detailed list of the fruit growing in Barbados and of that imported, but the planters had voiced the opinion that the land was too valuable for fruit production. Dried tamarind seed pods were the main export. They have a pleasant sweet/sour taste and are used in sauces and for a lemonade-type drink which is most refreshing on a very hot day. By 1888 Barbados was employing an analytical chemist and successful experiments were being conducted on sugar-cane. New types were being tried that were more resistant to disease and cane was being grown from seed, which was a new departure.

Dr Daniel Morris had been appointed as Director of Public Gardens and Plantations in Jamaica in 1879. In 1890 he visited Barbados as leader of the Royal Commission to investigate the state of the West Indies. By that time there was a botanical station of 90 acres at Dodd's Reformatory where the boys were used as labour. There were close ties with Jamaica to whom the Barbados establishment was affiliated. As a result of Morris' travels the Royal Commission issued a report in which they recommended the establishment of the headquarters of the Imperial Department of Agriculture in the West Indies at Barbados and further that Dr Morris should be the Commissioner. A conference was held in Barbados in 1899. The report of its proceedings makes clear that it wished to render assistance to all the sugar-producing colonies and in particular to

help improve production methods. Only one third of the population was working in the sugar industry and not all usable land was under cultivation. A lot of land was used for casual food crops in a most inefficient manner. Originally there had been only three botanical institutions in the Caribbean but by then there were 13. The report repeated the objectives of the establishments, i.e. experimental work, introducing new plants, propagating, distribution and training instructors. Agricultural shows and exhibitions were recommended as a method of education with prizes offered for good produce. Bulletins, handbooks and leaflets should also be produced as a form of instruction. Finally they recommended teaching about agriculture in primary and high schools as well as colleges and agriculture schools. These recommendations had far-reaching effects; even today in some of the islands some of these suggestions are still followed.

Today Barbados still grows sugar. The green waving mass still lines the roads but it does not dominate the economy any longer. There is a diversity of crops and tourism has taken its place.

The Morgan Lewis mill, Barbados. (Chris Huxley)

Gardens

❧ ANDROMEDA GARDENS ❧
ST JOSEPH (NATIONAL TRUST)

Andromeda Gardens are well-known amongst plantsmen. Not only are they very beautiful, they also have a tremendous collection of unusual plants from all over the world collected by Mrs Iris Bannochie who created the gardens. The site of the gardens is very striking. It is high above the sea and rocks of the east shore of Barbados and gets all the prevailing wind. Like other gardens in Barbados they are on a very steep hillside and have a stream running through which has been most imaginatively harnessed for use. The soil is a rich clay which in places is over thirty feet deep. The land has belonged to the McConney family since about 1740 and Mrs Bannochie inherited her share in 1953. The house was built soon after and the garden started at the same time.

The site is a very old one horticulturally. Excavation has turned up Arawak tools and other traces of previous cultivation. Like all the best gardens, it has grown gradually. There were other signs on the land of its previous use – trees of breadfruit (*Artocarpus altilis*) and coconut (*Cocos nucifera*), a large bearded fig or banyan (*Ficus citrifolia*) and fustic trees (*Chlorophora tinctoria*) There were whitewood trees (*Tabebuia pallida*), used for boat building, pop-a-gun trees (*Cecropia peltata*) which are medicinally useful, and small fruit trees such as guava (*Psidium guajava*), soursop (*Annona muricata*), custard apple (*Annona reticulata*), avocado (*Persea americana*), Barbados cherry (*Malphigia emarginata*) and *Agave barbadensis*, which is used in harvesting sea eggs or urchins, much relished locally.

In the summer of 1956 the daughters of the house persuaded their father and boyfriends to help them make a swimming pool. It took some weeks but the fill was used for a terraced garden and the area around the pool was also levelled and made into a lawn with the sloping area turned into an extension of the hibiscus garden. Great curtains of blue and white petrea hang down near the sitting area. The garden now covers six acres.

The layout of the gardens consists of small winding paths joining open areas of lawn or rooms, each one surrounded by collections of plants. The numerous boulders and rocks, far from making life difficult for Mrs Bannochie, to a certain extent actually dictated the planting. She started by pulling out the weeds in the crevasses and putting in plants instead. The needs of the plants were paramount in the planning of the gardens. A level area near the house was established to set it off and the hole thus made was turned into a lily pond, divided by a bridge. It has several types of lily including the Amazon lily (*Victoria amazonica*). There are several bridges across the stream and many paths zigzagging across the hillside. There are differing micro-climates and varying soil conditions in the gardens and grouping of plants needing similar cultural conditions was necessary. The result has been a series of gardens such as a heliconia garden, a hibiscus garden, an orchid garden and a palm garden.

As one enters by the main gate there is a shade house full of orchids, some hanging on the outside of the house.

There are orchids growing on trees all through the gardens and more are down in the more humid valley. A walk leads one up the hill through a shaded area with heliconias and torch lilies (*Etlingera elatior*) on either side. The shade that these need is provided by the bigger trees and as one climbs the hill there is a very handsome specimen of *Pandanus veitchii* (variegated) with a welcoming seat in its shade.

At the top of the path is a huge old ficus (*F. citrifolia*) surrounded by rocks all with their complement of plants in the crevasses. Below the ficus is another small lily pool with water-lilies and wandering jew (*Setcreasea purpurea*) on the edging rocks. Down the hill and to the right again is one of the hibiscus gardens. Below to the left are more orchids and then the palm garden. Here is the very large talipot palm (*Corypha umbraculifera*) which grows to a great height over about 60 years, puts out a giant inflorescence and then dies. There are some young ones as well. There is *Licuala grandis* with its large leaves and the sealing wax palm (*Cyrtostachys renda*) from Malaysia, so-named because of its bright red leaf bases and petioles. There is also a palm that almost looks like an animal with its hairy prickly trunk, the macaw palm (*Aiphanes erosa*), a fishtail palm (*Caryota mitis*) and some of the more usual palms like the Fiji fan palm (*Pritchardia pacifica*) and the date palm (*Phoenix* sp.)

Beyond the palm garden there is a buttercup tree (*Cochlospermum vitifolium*) which flowers in the spring before any leaves appear. The name is very suitable for the

The Amazonian lily, always a source of interest.

The screw pine (*Pandanus veitchii*).

blossoms are just like giant buttercups. Through a shady area one comes to the lily pool again. It is almost impossible to describe all the plants that crowd these gardens. It is interesting to remember that plants did not just come in from other parts of the world, they went out too, for Mrs Bannochie was a well-known collector and travelled widely to find her treasures. The gardens are now owned by the Barbados National Trust and are open every day. There is a garden guide and the plants are numbered to assist you.

Restaurant and shop. Open 8.00 am to sunset.
Telephone: 433–9384, 433–9261

❧ CODRINGTON COLLEGE ❧
ST PHILIP

In the parish of St Philip on the east coast in a peaceful, rather remote setting lies Codrington College. Its name comes from Christopher Codrington, a seventeenth-century planter who became Captain General and Governor of the Leeward Islands. This plantation was his home and the house of the Principal of the College would appear to date from the seventeenth century, the College buildings from the eighteenth century. The College was founded under his will of 1702 and opened in 1745 as a theological college and thus is the oldest seminary in the Western hemisphere and the first educational establishment in Barbados. It is a very peaceful place, approached by a handsome avenue of huge royal palms (*Roystonea* sp.) which must be very old. In front of the buildings is a large fish pond which may have been used as a holding tank for fish in the old way. In its time it served as the only swimming pool in Barbados but now it has different coloured water-lilies and it is the birds who come to fish. There are very large mahoganies (*Swietenia mahagoni*) in the grounds and standing on the lawns overlooking the sea are big white cedars (*Tabebuia pallida*) as well as a huge *Ficus citrifolia* near the Principal's house on the sea side. It is a place to visit in the quiet of the evening unless you want to watch the cricket played on the grassy area between the College and the road.

The old cedar tree and lily pond near the driveway into the College.

❧ FLOWER FOREST ☙
RICHMOND PLANTATION, ST JOSEPH

The countryside round Flower Forest is very steep and hilly, with deep clefts in the rocks, and very thickly wooded. The garden is on a steep hillside with winding paths and lovely views, both out across the valley which has many coconut palms standing out from the other woodland and to the east shore of Barbados with its cliffs and surf from the prevailing wind.

Originally the land was a farm which was much bigger than the present garden. It was a sugar plantation and there was coconut farming. It had become completely run down and neglected by the time it was purchased in 1980 by three men, one of whom was Richard Coghlan. He had designed other gardens in Barbados but this was to be his masterpiece. A lot of thought has been given for the visitor. The original building burned down in 1990 and this enabled a new building to be specially designed as a reception area, a shop and restaurant. But it has also been designed to facilitate movement of people and for wheelchair access. On occasions there are literally thousands there. The garden is big enough and spread out enough to take them because there are alternative route paths everywhere. The brochure has been translated into seven different languages. The labelling of the plants is good and comprehensive, both for the botanist and the average interested person. It is a matter of principle that no chemicals are used in the garden although there is a bad slug and snail problem. The only other 'pests' are the monkeys who

Begonias make a good contrast with brighter coloured flowers.

Heliconia growing beside the path.

eat the two-day pink hibiscus and swing about in the trees breaking branches, but they are tolerated with good temper.

The garden is designed into thickly planted areas bisected by paths which then lead on to a series of lawns, the idea being to have a series of 'rooms' each differently planted. The soil is heavy clay. The main 'bones' of the garden are formed from the larger trees which are evenly planted across the hillside. In fact these are arranged as various collections. Palms are one such, medicinal and useful trees, plants and shrubs others and fruit trees another. Fiji fan palm (*Pritchardia pacifica*), the fishtail palm (*Caryota mitis*), the macaw palm (*Aiphanes erosa*), the round leaf palm (*Licuala grandis*), the raffia palm (*Raphia farinifera*) and a large group of *Roystonea* sp. palms, *Sabal minor* and

Hoffman's palm are some of the constituents of this palm collection. Of the medicinal and useful trees there is the morinda or painkiller tree – 'dog dumpling' is its local name. There is the sapote or poison tree with its brown trunk and the sandbox tree (*Hura crepitans*) with its prickly trunk. Nearby is a self-sown seedling. Its common name comes from the seed pod which is round and hard and used to be filled with sand to be used as blotting paper to dry the ink from quill pens. Of useful trees there are soursop (*Annona muricata*) and avocado (*Persea americana*), cocoa (*Theobroma cacao*), banana (*Musa* sp.), mango (*Mangifera indica*) and the sweetly scented ylangylang (*Cananga odorata*), this last a component of perfumes. More 'useful' trees, shrubs or plants are the papyrus and pandanus from Cuba, *Aristolochia* (used for gripes and

Alpina purpurata, the red ginger, dramatic in its glowing colour.

snake bites) and *Allamanda cathartica*, now used in malaria control.

Then there are the purely ornamental trees. Down in the valley at the bottom of the garden are several African tulip trees (*Spathodea campanulata*). From the seat of one of the

lookouts the view is down on their red blossoms and out to the east shore in the distance. There are *Erythrina corallodendrum*, *Parkinsonia aculeata* and *Samanea saman*. All of these are underplanted with a wealth of plants. This planting is done in large groups of 30, 70 or more of the same plant.

Colour is also a consideration. From the building down into the garden extends an area devoted to pink flowers with two-day pink hibiscus, clerodendron, *Podranea ricasoliana* and *Graptophyllum pictum* 'Tricolor'. Further on is part of the collection of the 30 different heliconias in the garden including the red form from St Vincent, *H. bihai* and *H. caribaea* which is yellow. There is also a red ginger (*Alpinia purpurata*) and the large torch ginger (*Etlingera elatior*), plus the lovely pink *Alpinia purpurata rosea*. A collection of crotons is off down another little path – there are 70 different ones. There are several bushes of the strange Chinese hat bush (*Holmskioldia sanguinea*) and, as part of the low underplanting, there is a miniature bamboo that can be clipped to a small hedge which can be most effective. More plants used as underplanting are oxalis and purple heart (*Setcreasea purpurea*) and pileas. A large plant of the variegated *Pandanus veitchii* and also several bromeliads with their light pink and blue candles follow. In the light shade down the hillside are the collection of 4000 anthuriums, growing on the well-drained hillside on the usual bedding of coconut shell, and not far away is the purple orchid, *Bletia*. Back up the hill again are vanda orchids trained on to columns of coconut shell which is a very efficient medium. Near the top, cascading from large trees, are curtains of the thunbergia vine and below it on the slope the Tahiti gardenia. The path that connects the building to the car-park is planted with silver leaved plants and huge plants of brilliant bougainvillea, making a most effective entrance and exit from this lovely garden.

Restaurant and shop open daily
Telephone (Miss Helen Hill): 433–8152

FRANCIA PLANTATION
ST GEORGE

Francia is a working plantation of 50 acres, 26 of which are arable and the rest woods. The French grandfather of the present owner married a Barbadian girl and in 1910 they built the house and soon after laid out the garden. The area was pretty well bare coral rock with very little depth of soil so the terracing now to be seen was essential. The wind is very strong and frequent in Barbados so windbreaks are a necessity and must be established first, particularly as the house is built on an eminence just below the Gun Hill Signal Station. There was a lot of mahogany on the hillside and lower down jungly-type growth which was selectively cleared and under-planted with ferns. The garden owes much in its design to Edwin Lutyens with its urns, terraces and ponds which is not surprising considering its date. The approach to the house is up a long tree-lined drive (*Swietenia mahagoni*) which opens up to a large drive-around in front of the house with a circular lawn, a pond

The shade house at Francia which is useful for certain plants.

with a small fountain and, to one side, a shade house fronted by white begonias and red bougainvillea. There is a balustrade dividing the woodland from the drive with a row of urns with overflowing bougainvillea. A veranda runs the length of one side of the house, the pillars of which are covered in creeping ficus, and pots of ferns and orchids stand about. Below the veranda there is a lovely smooth, green lawn, most beautifully laid (it was originally a tennis lawn). Behind this is a pergola on which a very old pale purple bougainvillea is growing, so far unnamed, and a companion purple vine (*Pseudocalymma alliaceum*). There is a small pond with pretty ornamental lettuce (*Pistia stratiotes*) covering the water. The pool was discovered and re-dug out by the present owners. There are plans to extend this part of the garden; a large lawn has been made and a start made on planting exotic trees plus crotons. More bougainvillea divides this area. Over to the side of the garden are shaped beds full of different annuals and perennials such as verbena and alyssum, yellow iris and petunias. Miniature bamboo is used as edging. Two different colours of acalypha have been planted in small stone baskets. There is another shade house in this area with anthuriums, busy lizzies and dieffenbachias. Dividing the vegetable area from the ornamental garden is a hedge of *Plumbago capensis*. The old vegetable beds have to be used as cutting beds for flowers as the monkeys come down from the wood above to eat the produce. Here there are old fruit trees including a large mammy (*Mammea americana*) which has a big purple schomburgkia growing on it. There is also an orchard of mango trees (*Mangifera indica*) and yet more tubs of bougainvillea standing about. The

The little pond at Francia seen through an arch of purple and white bougainvillea.

old farm buildings are very compact and they and some very old huge tamarind trees (*Tamarindus indica*) divide the area of the big shade houses. These shade houses are used for growing the plants for the secondary business of the estate. Plants for renting out for offices, businesses and hotels are also grown here. Palms of various kinds, ficus and dieffenbachias are some of the varieties. One last feature which is very interesting is the viaduct which was built to drain the land after heavy rain. Because of the rocky surface the land floods very easily and this ingenious arrangement of a viaduct into a fluctuating pond was erected by the first owner.

The house and garden are open from Monday to Friday between 10.00 am and 4.00 pm.
Telephone (Mrs William Sisnott): 429–0474

HOTELS:
SANDY LANE, GLITTER BAY, ROYAL PAVILION
ST JAMES

These three hotels lie on the west coast of Barbados and represent a particular aspect of life in the island. Sandy Lane is older than the other two, built by the imagination and vision of Sir Ronald Tree and Robertson Ward, the well-known American architect in 1959. The coast here has many lovely sandy beaches and is sheltered from the prevailing wind. Ronald Tree was the first to discover the gold sand under its black covering of soot from a nearby sugar refinery. The building was designed in the Palladian style rather than the more popular Miami style in vogue at the time. Richard Coghlan was brought out from Kew Gardens to design and lay out the garden. Now he has made his name in the Caribbean as a gardener and designer and has written a practical book on gardening in the Caribbean.

On arrival at Sandy Lane the most noticeable feature is the very large, lovely old mahogany trees (*Swietenia mahagoni*). Growing in natural looking groups, they tower over the buildings and two particularly handsome specimens frame the view of the sea from the veranda of the reception area. The car-park has several poincianas (*Delonix regia*) round it and a lignum vitae (*Guaiacum officinale*) contributes its soft blue blossom. Paths lead down across lawns and the slope down to the reception area has been

The earliest part of the estate with the house.

161

This part of the garden runs between the two hotels.

terraced. Flights of steps lead down, broken at intervals by small paved areas in which there are fountains and small lily pools. Graceful palms give shade in front of the building and there are frangipani trees (*Plumeria*). Tubs of palms and begonias are dotted about.

Glitter Bay and Royal Pavilion are a bit further up the coast. The gardens of both were designed by Mr Tebora of Venezuela, who is also designing the new garden of the Royal Westmoreland Golf Club. Both are modern buildings but the property of Glitter Bay at one time belonged to the Cunard family. In fact it was in the original house of Glitter Bay that Sir Ronald Tree stayed when he first came to Barbados and conceived his idea for Sandy Lane. There is a separate building as a reception area for the hotel and this has been made the vehicle for a small courtyard type garden of pots containing crotons, pelargoniums and a lily pool, plus a separate pond with a fountain tinkling. As one leaves this area and walks toward the main hotel building, the restaurant on the beach and the pool area, there are many very tall coconut palms (*Cocos nucifera*). These are part of the original planting done by the Cunards. At the time they were the only available tree. The two gardens of Glitter Bay and Royal Pavilion bear the hallmarks of the same designer. In Glitter Bay garden there are large island beds with curving edges, one with dracaena under-planted with *Setcreasea purpurea*, huge great cycads, another large fountain, poinciana trees (*Delonix regia*), coconut palms and much lovely bougainvillea. Good use of the balconies of the hotel building has been made. Bougainvillea, white and

red, cascades down and yellow crotons peer over the edges. Out on the lawn between the two hotels large old trees were left to make part of the new garden, with poincianas and mahoganies, and there is a very large *Ficus citrifolia*.

Through the garden one comes to the garden of the Royal Pavilion. Here too are plants cascading from the verandas. There are several enclosed courtyards across the back of the hotel, away from the sea. Here there is a Spanish feeling to the architecture with its arches, tower and balconies. A clever device has been used – mirrors on the verandas to reflect the planting. There are large pots, each planted slightly differently; crotons in one, variegated pandanus in another, bougainvillea in another, and there are plants, including philodendron climbing up to the balconies. There are cycads in pots and aralias as well. The building is painted pink and a clever use of colour has been made with different sizes and colours of ixoras, also in pots, with pink and white frangipani planted in beds. On the sea side of the building, silver buttonwood (*Conocarpus erectus*) has been used to good effect with more bougainvillea and crinum lilies plus yuccas and again ixoras, coconut palms and poincianas. None of this planting is unusual in itself. There are no particularly rare plants, but the way the plants have been used is very pleasing in their effect.

The Spanish influence can be seen in this small wall fountain.

Hotel, restaurant and shop. Garden open to guests.
Telephone: 422–4111

163

❧ SUNBURY PLANTATION HOUSE ❧
ST PHILIP

The house of Sunbury is of a fairly modest size for a plantation house but as a museum it now contains a collection of handsome furniture and one of farm implements. At the front of the house, below the entrance steps, stands a large *Ficus citrifolia* under-planted with ferns and at the edge of the entrance drive are the remains of what would have been called a stone fence. It consists of a stone wall with pillars and wooden paling between the pillars, a very popular form of enclosure for private gardens in the seventeenth and eighteenth centuries. This is now almost hidden by a mixed hedging of palms, bougainvillea, petrea and acalypha. The garden is not very large but at the side of the house is a teak tree, presumably a remnant of the first teak planted in Barbados by Sir John Barrow in the eighteenth century. He also planted the mahogany trees (*Swietenia mahagoni*) at the end of the present garden. Three hundred were originally planted but only 130 still remain. They have been shaped by the wind and their grey trunks and dappled shade are interesting.

Restaurant and shop. Open daily 10.00 am to 5.00 pm.
Telephone: 423–6270

The old 'stone fence', as they were once called, at Sunbury.

VILLA NOVA
ST JOHN

The house of Villa Nova was one of the houses rebuilt after the devastating 1831 hurricane and completed in 1834. The property is of fourteen acres but there are six and a half acres of garden. The present garden is very lush and well grown. It was partly created by Mr and Mrs Ernest Hunte with the help of Iris Bannochie, the creator of the Andromeda Gardens on the east shore. Calm green curving lawns stretch away from the house, below its surrounding veranda, to a screen of large trees. There are carefully structured gaps in the barrier so that one may look out to the rolling countryside and the sea beyond. Like so many plantation houses, Villa Nova was built on high land to avoid the mosquito-ridden swamps, and away from the coast because of hurricanes.

There are large mahoganies (*Swietenia mahagoni*) in the garden as well as large poincianas (*Delonix regia*) and bauhinias, also a cannonball tree (*Couroupita guianensis*) with its interesting growth – the flowers come straight from the trunk and the leaves of the tree are only on its top half, quite separate. There are also royal palms (*Roystonea* sp.) and ebonies (*Albizia lebbeck*) and everything is underplanted with begonias, ferns and busy lizzies. There are small areas screened by vegetation, some paved with red tiles on which stand containers of ferns. Creepers climb up the big trees as well as orchids and ferns, and between the main garden and the swimming pool area is a citrus orchard. There is a charming old stable yard with large

A detail of the attractive garden at Villa Nova.

pots of bougainvillea and more creepers scrambling over the dividing wall.

The future of the house is to become a hotel – the main house will be the restaurant and hotel apartments are to be built in the far garden.

Restaurant and shop.
Open Monday–Friday 9.00 am to 4.00 pm.
Telephone: 433–1524

165

✄ WELCHMAN HALL GULLY ✄
ST THOMAS

This gully is in the parish of St Thomas in a high part of Barbados, about 900 ft above sea-level. There was once a series of caves in this area and in this case the roof of the caves fell in. Some of the rock formations on the side of the gully are interesting, and the coral formation can be clearly seen. The gully is fertile and boasts some 200 species of plants. The Barbados National Trust, which now owns the property, provide a good guide to some of these plants. It is a very pleasant, cool place to walk on a hot afternoon as it is so high and the gully is so shaded. The path from the car-park leads past great rocks standing like sentinels and a huge ficus tree (*F. citrifolia*). The area then opens out to a grassy area where great bamboos lean over from the wall of the gully. There is a lot of underplanting but the effects are very subtle. There are red heliconias with their colour picked up by the crotons which are more green than red on account of the shade. There are also many pink and white begonias. The path winds on down. It is a cool green quiet place with just the sound of ground doves cooing. In the early morning or late evening families of the Barbados green monkey can be seen.

Open daily 9.00 am to 5.00 pm.
Telephone: 438–6671
(Barbados National Trust: Telephone: 426–2421, 436–9033)

Tall coconut palms give shade.

SEVEN

TRINIDAD

Introduction and history

Trinidad is the largest of the islands of the southern Caribbean, approximately 50 miles from north to south and 50 miles from east to west. It was named by Columbus on his third voyage when he saw its three mountains in the south of the island. The remainder of the island is a low agricultural plain with the famous pitch lake in the south-west of the island. It lies off the coast of South America on the 10° line north of the Equator. The native flora is South American and it has a large population and range of bird species, giving it the nickname 'the land of the humming-bird'. Oil brought prosperity to Trinidad and enabled it to take a different path from the other islands of the Caribbean. Although it relied on agriculture in its early years, now its biggest export is oil and petroleum products and, although tourists are welcome, it has turned its face

The chaconia (*Warszowicazia coccinea*), the national flower of Trinidad. (Michael Bourne)

against mass tourism. There is still a certain amount of marvellously wild, heavily-wooded countryside in the north of the island. Great Britain united Trinidad and Tobago politically in 1898 when both were colonies.

The first Europeans to see the island were the Spanish as they passed in their galleons on the way to South America. It was occupied at that time by the Arawaks. When the Caribs arrived it was the only island which they both inhabited. Together they fought off European settlement for a hundred years.

The first settlers were Spanish but they had only a small garrison as Trinidad was regarded as a defensive outpost and there were just a few settlers to use the fertile land. A small quantity of tobacco was grown. By the beginning of the seventeenth century it was being used as a setting-off point for expeditions to South America to search for gold. The Dutch also had small settlements there. Until the latter part of the eighteenth century it seems to have had a quiet existence and little mention is made of it. In 1783 the Spanish king tried to encourage settlement and grants of land were given to people who were allies of Spain. When the French Revolution took place and spread to the French colonies people fled from Haiti and San Domingo and one of the places they went to was Trinidad. There they set up cocoa and sugar plantations. They also established coffee plantations – by the time Britain took over the island in 1797 there were 130 of them. The British tried to encourage sugar cultivation but it was a turbulent time as the population was so mixed with different nationalities.

Gardening climate

Trinidad has a tropical climate with a high degree of humidity. There is a pronounced dry season from January to mid-May, when it is also cooler, with an average temperature of 30°C. From mid-May onwards it is warmer, with a maximum temperature of 32°C. The island has an overall average rainfall of 70 inches annually. There are three chains of mountains, the Northern Range, the Central Range and the Southern Range, with a higher rainfall than on the flat or undulating terrain. The mountains determine the drainage pattern of the rivers.

Gardening soils

There are three main rivers in Trinidad. The Caroni river flows between the Northern and Central Ranges across the Caroni plain. The land in this area is very flat and floods in the rainy season. This is an area of mangrove and other trees and shrubs. The low-lying plains are the main agricultural areas. The soils here are alluvial, containing a mixture of humus, sand, silt, clay and minerals. Flooding can lead to erosion. Sugar-cane, fruits and vegetables grow well. Trinidad also has petroleum and large reserves of natural gas, iron ore (which is unexploited) and the world's largest supply of natural asphalt in the Pitch Lake.

Garden history

In 1818 it was decided by the Trinidad government to establish a botanic garden in Trinidad. An abandoned sugar estate north of Port of Spain was purchased. It also

Mangroves support a whole eco-system and protect the sandy shores.

had a house suitable for a Governor's residence. The house was put in a good state of repair and Sir Ralph Woodford, the Governor, moved in. The gardens, approximately 63 acres in all, were laid out round the house. Plants were brought from St Vincent to help establish the garden, and the first botanist in charge, Mr Lockhart, travelled to Venezuela and other countries of the Orinoco delta to collect. He brought many orchids back as well as saman (*Samanea saman*) and cow trees (*Brosimum utile*). He also introduced various spice trees.

In 1834 slaves were emancipated and this had the same traumatic effect in Trinidad as it did elsewhere in the Caribbean. Many left the work on the plantations and moved into the towns but others stayed in the country and farmed their own small plots. There had been free villages before emancipation as there were in Jamaica. However large stretches of land were still uncultivated so the government encouraged immigration. In 1845 the first indentured Indians arrived. The following year the Sugar Equalisation Act was passed in England which in effect removed the protective tariffs on West Indian sugar. In many of the islands planters could not compete and went bankrupt (this was also because the industry was so unmechanised and old-fashioned in its methods). Luckily Trinidad introduced new tools and methods to economise on labour and reduce production costs. Trinidad and British Guiana became the two most progressive territories.

By the 1880s concern for the economic well-being of the West Indies in general was being felt in England. Sugar beet grown in Europe was taking the place of sugar and some of the other crops could be grown better and less expensively in other countries. Two Royal Commissions, in 1882 and 1896, recommended diversification of crops and in particular the growing of fruit. In tandem with this, departments of agriculture were to set up and botanical gardens established in many of the islands. These gardens were to vary in size and according to that were either stations or gardens. Trinidad had an experimental station which fulfilled one of the objects of the scheme: experimentation with new strains of existing crops and the establishment of new ones. The results were to be distributed to farmers and instruction in new methods was also to be available.

The diversity of what did grow in Trinidad is confirmed by some visitors' accounts. Charles Kingsley visited in 1869 and spent Christmas in the building known as The Cottage near the entrance to the Botanical Gardens. Government House had fallen into disrepair again (probably a victim of termites, a common problem with wooden houses) and this building was used by the Governor for some years until further repairs were done. His ecstatic descriptions of the variety and exuberance of the plant life make interesting reading, this in spite of an appalling fire that had raged the year before over a very large area.

In 1884 Lady Brassey and a party on a large yacht sailed into Trinidad on a journey that took them to several islands in the Caribbean and to Venezuela, with the family dogs. (She published her account in a limited private edition but with no explanation as to the reason for the expedition or any personal details.) Her first impression was of the luxuriant growth of the *virgin tropical forest*. She saw plantations

The strange dragon tree is a native of Madeira and the Canary Islands.

were dramatic and there were plenty of hibiscus, allamanda, caladium and begonias in the shade. She saw the silk cotton tree which stood at the gates of the garden, breadfruit and jujubes. She visited the botanical garden with the curator, Mr Prestoe, and said the garden was divided into three parts: a flower garden, arboretum and palmetum as well as an orchard and *economic ground*. In the last were nutmeg and different coffees being grown and there was a nursery, presumably for the distribution of plants to the local planters. In this nursery were croton, bamboo, mango, gum trees, malacca apple trees, plantains, vanilla orchids, 'peach' palm, oil palm and cacao. Her comment was *a good deal of attention being paid to improve the cultivation of cacao*; 13 000 000 lbs worth £500 000 was being exported annually as well as 144 000 lbs of coffee. She said the walks about the garden were well laid out and the *trees judiciously planted* and she lists cinnamon, calabash, 'vegetable ivory' (*Phytelephas macrocarpa*), Brazil nut (*Bertholletia excelsa*), cannonball tree and a pandanus collection.

The party visited Government House both for dinner and to stay as a respite from the yacht. She describes the house as being *in the midst of the Gardens* with wonderful flowering creepers covering the verandas – bougainvillea, *Aristolochia trilobata*, jasmine, stephanotis and allamanda all scrambling together to give extra shade. Another fact that impressed her favourably was the coolness of that house and others she visited. The through draughts and verandas made it cooler than some houses in London in the summer and the bareness of the furnishings contributed to this as well as not harbouring insects. While

of sugar-cane, coconut and coffee and noted aloes, yuccas and dragon trees. These last are natives of Madeira and the Canary Islands and are seldom seen out of that island. She saw an avenue of almond trees and one wonders if she meant the West Indian almond, rather than the European one. The orange, red and purple crotons and dracaena

Orcidium.

Thunbergia mysorensis.

This splendidly exotic display of orchids will grow in Trinidad.

Vanda hybrid.(Michael Bourne)

there she received a lovely present from Mr Prestoe, the curator, when he brought a great basket of orchids and flowers amongst which were phalaenopsis, the brown slipper orchid and the 'Holy Ghost' orchid. Another present included avocado pears and tomatoes as well as other vegetables.

Lady Brassey and her party took a long drive out into the countryside to visit the estate of Sir Joseph Needham. He had been working for years to improve the land and was then growing orange, lemon, shaddock, pomelo, passion flower, vanilla, tamarind, yams, sweet potato, arrowroot, cassava (also known as manioc), plus sugar-cane and coffee. Once again she was impressed by the lushness of growth. They passed through miles of savannah-like country with *fine herds of Cattle* and miles and miles of cacao plantations. She commented that in spite of cocoa, sugar and vanilla all being grown there was no chocolate manufacture on the island but all components were being sent to France.

They also passed many small houses belonging to ex-slaves. Each one had its own garden containing bananas, arrowroot, yams, manioc, malacca apple (which has magenta flowers like bottle brushes), and they passed a market where each person was selling his or her own produce which included chillies, oranges, mangoes, carrots, salads, sugar apple, cherimoya, and pineapples. On arrival at Sir Joseph's estate they were served most delicious drinks and food and she noted the wonderful different timbers that were used in the construction of the house – mahogany and cedar amongst others.

It was soon after Lady Brassey's departure that the scheme to set up botanical gardens and stations in as many islands of the Caribbean as possible was mooted. Trinidad got no funding for its garden from the Imperial Government but was well on the way and had its own analytical chemists. The *Gardeners' Chronicle* of November 1897 reporting on the West Indies Commission made the following comment about Trinidad:

Between 1887 and 1896 over 285 000 plants and 123 000 packets of seed have been distributed. At present it is evident that too much time of the superintendent is occupied in the cultivation and distribution of plants of an ornamental character and in maintaining flower beds and borders around Government House. Furthermore the present garden is too small the soil generally too poor for the successful cultivation of economic plants. It is recommended that land be obtained elsewhere purely for an experimental agricultural station.

After these rather grudging and critical comments another article appeared in the *Gardeners' Chronicle* of August 1900 giving the information that all botanical and experimental work was to be transferred to the St Clair experimental station. Nothing was to be removed from the old garden but representatives were to be placed at St Clair under more modern systems of classification. *The old garden in which the Governor's residence is situated will be kept up as an ornamental garden.* It also noted that the Tobago experimental station was under the direction and immediate control of the Trinidad Garden. In 1908 Trinidad got its Department of Agriculture and in 1922 the Imperial College of Tropical Agriculture took over the work of the department. Finally in 1960 that became the Faculty of Agriculture of the University of the West Indies.

Gardens

❧ BOTANIC GARDENS ❧
PORT OF SPAIN

The gardens are north of the large grass area known as the Savannah on the outskirts of Port of Spain. Originally the land was a sugar estate and was purchased by Government in 1816. The gardens opened two years later. The Savannah is an imposing area of grass with large ornamental trees on the edge of it and seven interesting houses with varying architectural styles on the other side of the road (purported to be the largest roundabout in the world). The gardens occupy an area with a rise on one side, a gentle hill, and the remainder flat. Government House, which is now the President's House, still stands on its original site, but in its private garden. Originally the garden at 63 acres was larger than it is today. Now it gives land to headquarters buildings for the garden and a small zoo. During the dry weather, which lasts four months early in the year, the grass becomes extremely brown and dried up and the herb garden has to be resown annually.

At the entrance to the gardens is a great spreading saman tree (*Samanea saman*) covered in the yellow cat's claw vine (*Macfadyena unguis-cati*) and the entrance gate is draped in the garlic vine (*Pseudocalymma alliaceum*) with its delicate blue flowers. A cyp or cypre (*Cordia alliodora*), a native tree, is nearby. Many of the trees in the garden are very old, including a logwood (*Haematoxylum campechianum*) which the bees love. Parallel to the road is the palm

The palm walk in the Botanic Gardens is depicted in many of the old prints of the gardens.

walk which still has a very good collection of palms, as when Charles Kingsley visited it in 1869. Two big branching date palms (*Phoenix dactylifera*) are followed by the wax palm (*Copernicia cerifera*) from which record wax came. There are royal palms and the Cuban royal palm (*Roystonea* sp.) The first has its bulge at the young stage, the second in its middle. A betel palm from which the betel nut comes, the 'chewing gum' of India is next, and of the same genus *Areca triandra*. Two species of fan palm (*Pritchardia thurstonii* and *P. pacifica*) follow and then two seedlings of *Livistona australis*. Two species of the fishtail palm (*Caryota mitis*) are accompanied by the itching palm and the manila palm. On the corner where paths meet is a *Ficus citrifolia* and beyond a small variety of the sabal palm (*S. maritima*). Sabal palms of other genera grow in both Florida and Bermuda. The cohune palm which provides cooking oil is there and the sealing wax palm (*Cyrtostachys renda*), so named for its red trunk. It can be propagated by its spreading root which develops shoots, but it does not like the dry periods. In spite of this impressive list, Mr Bhorai Kalloo would like more species. The remaining species are the prickly palms with their prickly trunks and the windmill palm (*Chamaerops excelsa*). Further along the path there is a very old eucalyptus, which is the type that gives the medicinal oil, and a Jamaican wattle.

The lawns open out and all across them, planted at *judicious intervals*, as Lady Brassey wrote, are various large and decorative trees. There is also an avenue of old bay rum trees (*Pimenta racemosa*), described by visitors in the last century. There is a bloodwood (*Pterocarpus indicus*) and a big old *Tamarindus indica*, a coum palm and another ficus

These bay rum trees are very old.

(*F. religiosa*), the peepul tree regarded as sacred in the Far East. The eucalyptus tree here gives citron oil – the bark is a most lovely dappled one of several colours. Nearby is the great spreading umbrella of a black ebony.

The hillside is reserved for native species. Amongst other trees are the monkey ear (*Enterolobium cyclospermun*) so called from the shape of its pod and seen often also in Jamaica. The ginep (*Melicoccus bijugatus*) is a native of Guyana and there is a very old climbing blue petrea as well as jacarandas and bauhinias. The small graveyard in the centre of the large lawn is where past governors and botanists of the gardens are buried. The oldest part of the garden is over near the border which runs along the edge of the President's garden and contains the first introductions, including a very tall prunus, oldest of all. Here are several species of brownea and coffee trees (both the Liberian and the Arabian kind). There are also the jak fruit (*Artocarpus heterophyllus*), a relative of breadfruit from Asia, a Brazilian rubber tree (from the first introduction of rubber to Trinidad) and the raw beef tree, named for the colour of its wood when cut. Other useful trees are the mangosteen, the Jamaican walnut, African mahogany, nutmeg (*Myristica fragrans*) and roucou (*Bixa orellana*) which is used to colour margarine, cheese and other dairy products. These are part of the very good collections of the past which also include ginger, lychee and the chaconia (*Warszewiczia coccinea*). Its blossom, vermilion in colour, is the national flower of Trinidad. It grows on the edge of the forest in the wild.

There is a large shade house in this area where such plants as orchids, caladiums and spathiphyllums are

More of the collection of palms in the gardens.

grown. Nearby is a huge pink poui (*Tabebuia pentaphylla*), lending its shade to the house. The Norfolk Island pine (*Araucaria bidwillii*) has an edible nut regarded as a local speciality.

From this incomplete list it can be seen that the Botanical Gardens were very splendid in the past and indeed seem so now. It would also be good if further introductions could be made, particularly of plants that are now endangered in the wild. The work of botanical gardens the world over is changing to preservation of endangered species rather than the collection of curiosities as it was in the past.

As always, money and priorities of governments are the indeterminate factor.

Two useful addresses:

The Garden Club of Trinidad & Tobago
P.O. Box 205
Port of Spain, Trinidad

The Horticultural Society of Trinidad & Tobago
P.O. Box 252
Port of Spain, Trinidad

Private gardens

MRS RITA BARROW
VALSAYN NORTH

This is an amazingly colourful garden, not only for its yellow and reds but for its variegated plants. It is a completely flat area but varying interest has been achieved with large trees, shaped borders and central interest on the lawn. Near the entrance on either side of the drive are low hedges of the miniature ixora in red and yellow, kept clipped neatly like a box hedge in Europe. There is also an edging of variegated aralia kept clipped, and low and in front of the house is a slightly higher bed of blue *Plumbago capensis*. Screening the road is a long border in which are variegated hibiscus, croton, acalypha and lantana. Giving height is a grouping of pandanus, fronted by variegated aloe and a yellow cordyline in front again. A variegated ficus has been trained into a formal ball. *Pachystachys lutea* from Peru, which is yellow, alternates with red crotons and the blue of *Plumbago capensis* and there are variegated orange heliconias, which are also low. Across the width of the garden at one end are fruit trees: sapodilla (*Manilkara zapota*) and mangoes (*Mangifera indica*). The mango trees play host to various orchids, *Oncidium luridum* being one, and ferns. There are a very big adiantum, a pink philodendron and dendobriums on a bottle brush tree (*Callistemon lanceolatus*). There is also a bromeliad garden in the corner under the shade of a variegated *Ficus triangularis*. Here there are also the bromeliad *Aechmea dichlamydea*

A collection of yellow and red miniature ixoras.

A little pond tucked away amongst the plants.

and its variant *A. trinitensis*. Under some of the big trees are the pots for propagating such things as crotons, and also pink and white anthuriums, *A. andraeanum* being one. There is a shade house with *Solandra guttata* climbing over it. Inside are bromeliads such as cryptanthus and aroids such as scindapsus. The tri-coloured croton 'King of Siam' is to be found here and there is a miniature variegated pandanus.

Round the back of the house there is another large full border and a tiny pond almost hidden in the large plants and the ferns surrounding it. In this border are an episcia which has a variegated leaf and red flowers and the bougainvillea from Brazil with its two-coloured flowers of purple and white with variegated leaves. There are also several variations of acalypha and some lovely large ixoras with the white mussaenda as contrast plus a most prosperous *Asparagus myerii* backed by sealing wax palms (*Cyrtostachys renda*) with their red trunks.

The house itself has an inner courtyard with its own planting bed. In here are more crotons, dieffenbachia and small palms.

> Visits for specialist groups to this can be arranged through the local travel agents or the Garden Club (P.O. Box 205, Port of Spain) and some notice would be appreciated.

The owner has a great preference for variegated plants.

MR AND MRS RODNEY DE BOEHMLER
HALELAND PARK, PORT OF SPAIN

This house and garden stands in Haleland Park, a pleasant suburban area of Port of Spain so the area of the garden is not very large compared to some others, but very clever use has been made of the land available. The garden at the front of the house has been formed into a miniature landscape with a tiny hill making a slope on the lawn and what appears to be a stream winding its way through the garden with a small pond. A black olive tree gives shade to the lawn and tall heliconias screen the road as well as variegated alpinia at the back of the pond. In the pond is the water lettuce (*Pistia stratiotes*) and an aroid which is native to Trinidad. Along the boundary fence is a hibiscus hedge fronted by pink heliconia and pigeon pea (*Cajanus cajan*) and an ink berry has been trained to trail gracefully over the pond. Following the course of the stream as edging plants are ferns and busy lizzies backed by *Heliconia pendula* from Venezuela, variegated heliconias and alpinia 'Eileen McDonald' which is pink. There is also the yellow shrimp plant (*Beloperone guttata*). The stream goes all the way down this side of the garden.

At the back of the house the land has been narrowly terraced with beds of roses, very interesting as it is so hot in Trinidad. There are also many tables of bonsai plants, another interest of Mr de Boehmler's, and large cages with many canaries and finches. The bonsai specimens include some original efforts such as a ficus and different species of

An attractive way to train bougainvillea in a limited space.

pine and the yellow chinese hat plant (*Holmskioldia sanguinea*). Also in this part of the garden is a pool with a shady sitting out area with hanging baskets of ferns and a garlic vine (*Pseudocalymma alliaceum*) climbing up the boundary fence. The planting includes yellow and red

One of the owner's great passions is bonsai.

crotons, red ixora and a very large variegated crinum plus six different heliconias. The land slopes away down the back of the garden and there are some fruit trees, oranges and other citrus and bananas, to form a little orchard. One unusual fruit tree from the Far East is Pomme cythere (*Spondias cytherea*). The path leading down is edged with Easter lilies (*Lilium longiflorum*) and terminates with a small shade house for propagating. The wealth of plants in this comparatively small area and the clever landscaping is what attracts one's admiration.

Telephone (Mr and Mrs Rodney de Boehmler): 629–2192

180

❧ MRS HOLDER ❧
NEW TOWN, PORT OF SPAIN

This is a very small town garden (in New Town, Port of Spain) in the European tradition. It comprises an L-shaped area in front and at the side of an old house with traditional wooden shutters of Trinidad. The area has been tiled with terracotta and there is a narrow border against the wall. However into this very small area has been fitted both palmetto (*Sabal* sp.), fan palms (*Livistona chinensis*) and a McArthur palm of Philippine origin plus a fishtail palm (*Caryota mitis*). A traveller's palm (*Ravenala madagascariensis*) rises above them all. Pots have been used to good effect, one containing a peach coloured datura, another a *Tabernaemontana* sp. with gardenia-like flowers, another spider plants. There are in the narrow border two very handsome *Mussaenda erythrophylla*, one a dark pink, the other a pale pink, 'Queen Sirikit', and a purple bauhinia. Room has also been made for a carambola or star fruit (*Averrhoa carambola*) and an orange. Climbing up the fence are a garlic vine (*Pseudocalymma alliaceum*), the Barbados flower fence (*Caesalpinia pulcherrima*) and a combretum vine which has flowers that start orange and turn to red. By the gate are large torch lilies (*Etlingera elatior*) with their exotic flowers. In the shadows stands a life-size figure of a girl, her soft grey colouring merging into the greenery.

Mrs Holder is very pleased to show her garden but would like a telephone call first. Telephone: 622–2040.
(Her husband, Boscoe Holder, is an artist.)

A statue of a girl in a cool position in the garden.

DR AND MRS CLAYTON PROCOPE
ST AUGUSTINE

Mrs Procope is a very enthusiastic plantswoman and this shows in her garden with its many imported plants, most of which have come from the Far East. Their first introduction to Trinidad was to this garden. The garden which is a completely flat and smooth plot, stands behind a tall surrounding wall, in many places covered in the climbing miniature ficus. This gives a great sense of privacy and quiet. The house has a courtyard area with steps leading down to the garden. Within this area is colourful planting of balsam for the summer and red and yellow poinsettia for the winter months. There is a small pool planted with the miniature papyrus and a bed of bromeliads, *Dracaena* 'Tricolour' and aechmeas nearby. There is also a parrot's cage with an equally colourful inhabitant. Down on the lawn to the right is a group of trees, one a huge old mango (*Mangifera indica*) and a little spring and stream with stepping stones. Edging this area is a white scented ixora, white brunfelsia, a miniature variegated aralia (*Polyscias*) of Philippine origin and dieffenbachia and white impatiens spilling on to the lawn. In the shade of the trees are staghorn ferns, *Platycerium* sp. and orchids. One of the big trees is a mangosteen which fruits in November and under it are the big dark leaves of the alocasia.

Away from this cool, dark green shade the next area to catch attention is a herb garden. The smells and scents are the same as in Europe but the plants are different! To the right, edging the drive are big pots containing bougainvillea,

A colourful entrance to the garden – and a parrot.

Different shades of green – variegated aralia immediately, dieffenbachia, white ixora and white impatiens.

An interesting way of growing orchids.

group of sealing wax palms (*Cyrtostachys renda*) with their bright red trunks. A double *Allamanda cathartica* scrambles nearby. Along another boundary a curving border has been made. An ashoka tree from Thailand with its strange drooping branches and a pink jatropha, also from Thailand, plus an unusual tricoloured variegated hibiscus from Singapore, a white petrea and a dwarf grey leaved allamanda grow here. In the corner stands a lignum vitae (*Guaiacum officinale*) which has such wonderful blue blossoms. As it does not grow enormous, it makes a good garden tree. There is also a lychee and a yellow poui (*Tabebuia rufescens*) – the last is often used as street planting but is no less beautiful for that. There are schomburgkias attached to some of the trees, the cat's claw vine (*Macfadyena unguis-cti*) on the boundary fence and the night blooming cereus has its place with the *Agave americana variegata* and the screwpine (*Pandanus*) in a dry spot. There is also a large variegated pigeon pea (*Cajanus cajan*) and a large cycad, purportedly one of the oldest plant forms on earth.

one 'Miss Manilla', a lipstick pink, another 'Thimma' with pink and white bracts and yellow and green leaves from Thailand. This is an example of a first introduction to Trinidad by Mrs Procope. On the lawn are small pots growing various orchids – vandas and phalaenopsis. Nearby there is a big shade house full of ferns and palms and various treasures like more orchids needing its shade, bromeliads and guzmania. Beyond the shade house is a group of trees – a very big and old ylangylang (*Cananga odorata*) with its sweetly scented flowers, a component in perfume, a *Mussaenda erythrophylla* Queen Sirikit and a

> Mrs Procope is prepared to show her garden (on the eastern side of the University) to specialist groups and real plantspeople. Contact her directly, giving a bit of notice. Telephone: 662–4107

 ASA WRIGHT NATURE CENTRE

Essentially a bird and wildlife reserve with luxuriant tropical planting

GAZETTEER OF GARDENS
OPEN TO THE PUBLIC
ON OTHER ISLANDS

Cuba

JARDIN BOTANICO NACIONAL DE CUBA
CARRETERA DEL ROCIO, HAVANA

A well-maintained garden with excellent collections. It also has a Japanese garden.

JARDIN BOTANICO SOLEDAD
CIENFUEGOS

Contains a collection of Cuba's native plants.

THE ORCHIDARIUM
SOROA

Features over 700 orchid varieties.

Bermuda

BERMUDA BOTANICAL GARDENS
SOUTH ROAD, PAGET

A 36-acre garden of sub-tropical flora, an orchid house, an aviary, formal gardens, a hibiscus garden, a palm garden, a sub-tropical garden, a sub-tropical fruit garden and a garden for the blind.
(The Bermuda Garden Club organises visits to private gardens each year during March and April.)

Bahamas

NASSAU BOTANIC GARDENS
NASSAU, NEW PROVIDENCE

An 18-acre garden of sub-tropical plants.

The Joseph Reynold O'Neal Botanical Gardens in Tortola. (Chris Huxley)

Tortola

 BOTANICAL GARDENS
ROAD TOWN

Established to conserve and display much of the flora of
the islands.

❧ THE RETREAT ☙
VILLAGE ROAD, NASSAU, NEW PROVIDENCE

An 11-acre botanical park which is the headquarters of the Bahamas National Trust.

❧ HYDROFLORA GARDENS ☙
EAST BEACH DRIVE, FREEPORT, GRAND BAHAMA

Four acres of tropical plants grown hydroponically.

❧ THE GARDEN OF GROVES ☙
MAGELLAN DRIVE, FREEPORT

A 12-acre botanical garden around the Grand Bahama Museum.

Cayman Islands

❧ QUEEN ELIZABETH II ☙
BOTANIC GARDEN
GRAND CAYMAN

Developed since 1990, it now comprises a 0.8. mile long natural woodland walking trail and a Foliage Display Garden, the first of many display gardens which are planned.

❧ HYATT-REGENCY GRAND CAYMAN ☙
HOTEL

The Hyatt Regency hotel chain is well known for the extensive landscape gardens which have been developed around its hotels in tropical parts of the world.

Dominican Republic

❧ JARDIN BOTANICO NATIONAL ☙
URBANIZACION LOS RIOS, SANTO DOMINGO

A complete collection of endemic plants, the national herbarium, an aquatic plant pavilion, a Forest Ravine, a floral clock and a Japanese garden.

Puerto Rico

❧ THE BOTANICAL GARDEN, ☙
UNIVERSITY OF PUERTO RICO
RIO PIEDRAS, SAN JUAN

The 140-acre botanical park includes a large palmetum and an Institute of Tropical Forestry

Entrance to the Botanic Gardens, Grand Cayman

❧ THE BOTANICAL GARDEN, ❧
MAYAGUEZ

A tropical agricultural research station with a very large collection of tropical economic plants.

Guadeloupe

❧ JARDIN BOTANIQUE DE BASSETERRE ❧
RUE VICTOR HUGUES, BASSETERRE

A small but attractive botanic garden.

The garden of the Hyatt Regency Hotel, Grand Cayman

The yellow poui (*Cybistax donnelli-smithii*), often used as street planting in the Caribbean.

Martinique

 JARDIN DE BALATA
BALATA

From the point of view of design, one of the most interesting tropical gardens in the world.

PLANTATION DE LEYRITZ
BASSE POINTE

Sixteen acres of elegantly laid-out tropical gardens around an eighteenth-century stone greathouse.

MACINTOSH PLANTATION
MORNE ROUGE

A commercial cut-flower nursery with an extensive recently landscaped garden.

Guyana

 BOTANICAL GARDENS
GEORGETOWN

Over 100 acres of tropical gardens with many decorative Victorian garden features.

Victoria regis waterlily, Antigua. (Chris Huxley)

Select bibliography

Anderson, Alexander, 'An Account of The Botanic Garden of the Island of St Vincent' *Transactions of the Society of Arts*, London, 16.1798.

Anglerius, P.M., *The History of Travels in the West and East Indies*, London, 1577.

Aspinall, Algernon E., *The British West Indies*, 1912.

Bannochie, Iris, and Light, Marilyn, *Gardening in the Caribbean*, Macmillan, 1993.

Binney, Marcus, Harris, John and Martin, Kit, *Jamaica's Heritage*, The Mill Press, Jamaica, 1991.

Bourne, M.J., Lennox, G.W., and Seddon, S.A., *Fruits and Vegetables of the Caribbean*, Macmillan, 1988.

Brassey, Lady, *In the Trades, the Tropics and Roaring Forties*, 1885.

Coghlan, Richard, *Landscape Gardening in the Tropics*, 1973.

Coleridge, Henry Nelson, *Six Months in the West Indies*, London, 1825.

Desmond, Ray, *Bibliography of British and Irish Botanists and Horticulturalists*, Taylor, London, 1994.

Edwards, Bryan, *History Civil and Commercial of the British West Indies*, Dublin, 1819.

Eyre, Alan, *The Botanic Gardens of Jamaica*, Andre Deutsch Ltd., London, 1966.

Fermor, Patrick Leigh, *The Traveller's Tree*, Penguin, London, 1984.

Fraser, Antonia, *Oliver Cromwell – Our Chief of Men*, Methuen, 1973.

Grove, Richard H., *Green Imperialism*, Cambridge University Press, 1995.

Guide to Botanical Garden, Trinidad.

Guide to Dominica's Botanic Gardens.

Guilding, Rev. Lansdown, *Account of the Botanic Garden in the Island of St Vincent*, Glasgow, 1825.

Hargreaves, Dorothy and Bob, *Tropical Trees*, Hargreaves, 1965.

Heine, Heino, 'Tour of Jamaica', *International Dendrology Society Yearbook*, 1988.

Honychurch, Lennox, *The Dominica Story*, Macmillan, 1995.

Honychurch, Penelope, *Caribbean Wild Plants and their Uses*, Macmillan, 1986.

Howard, R.A., 'A History of the Botanical Garden of St Vincent, British West Indies', *The Geographical Review*, 1972.

Howard, Richard, *Early Botanical Records from the West Indies particularly Barbados*, 1979.

Hoyos, F.A., *Barbados – Our Island Home*, Macmillan, Fourth edition, 1989.

Hulme, Peter, and Whitehead, Neil, *Wild Majesty*, Clarendon Press, Oxford, 1992.

Journal of the Kew Guild, Royal Botanic Gardens, Kew, 1896, 1902–6, 1922.

Kew Bulletin, Royal Botanic Gardens, Kew, 1879–1908, 1923.

Kingsley, Charles, *At Last – A Christmas in the West Indies*, Macmillan, 1871.

Le Corre, Gildes, and Exbryat, Andre, *Flowers of the Tropics*, Editions Exbryat, Fort-de-France, Martinique, 1985.

Lennox, G.W. and Seddon, S.A., *Flowers of the Caribbean*, Macmillan, 1978.

Ligon, Richard, *A True and Exact History of the Island of Barbadoes*, 1657, Frank Cass & Co. Reprint, 1970.

J.C. Loudon, *The Encyclopaedia of Gardening*, London, 1824, 1835, 1871.

Morris, Dr. Daniel, 'Kew Men and Botanical Work in the Colonies', *Journal of the Kew Guild*, Royal Botanic Gardens, Kew, 1890.

Nelson, Dr. E.C., *Proceedings and Reports Belfast Natural History and Philosophical Society*, Belfast, Vol 10, 1977–82.

North, Marianne, *A Vision of Eden*, Webb and Bower, 1980.

Pattullo, Polly and Baptiste, Anne Jno, *The Gardens of Dominica*, Croton Press, 1998.

Pertchik, Bernard and Harriet, *Flowering Trees of the Caribbean*, Rinehart & Co, New York, 1951.

Peterkin, Joshua, *A Treatise on Planting*, St Kitts, 1790.

Powell, Dulcie, *The Botanic Garden, Liguanea*, The Institute of Jamaica, 1972.

Powell, Dulcie, *The Voyage of The Plant Nursery, HMS Providence, 1791–1793*, The Institute of Jamaica, 1973.

Reports of the Agricultural Department, Barbados.

'Report on Botanic Station, Dominica', *Leeward Islands Gazette*, 1892.

Schaw, Janet, *The Journal of a Lady of Quality (1774–6)*, Yale University Press, 1939.

Showker, Kay, *The Outdoor Traveller's Guide to the Caribbean*, New York, Stuart, Taboori And Chang, 1989.

Sloane, Hans, *A Voyage to the Islands of Madeira, Barbados, Nevis, St Christopher's and Jamaica*, 1707 and 1725.

Smith, John, *The True Travels, Adventures and Observations of Capt. John Smith between 1593 and 1629*, Messrs. Churchill, London, 1732.

The Garden Section of the Women's Club of Havana, *Flowering Plants from Cuban Gardens*, Havana, 1951.

The Gardeners' Chronicle, London, 1890–1893, 1897–1899, 1902–1904.

The Gardeners' Magazine, London, Nov. 8, 1890.

Trollope, Anthony, *The West Indies and the Spanish Main*, London, 1859.

Webster, Aimee, *Caribbean Gardening*, Jamaica, 1964.

Wood, H.T., *A History of the Society of Arts*,

Titles of related interest

Bermuda's Botanical Wonderland: A Field Guide
Christine Phillips-Watlington, 1996, Macmillan Caribbean

Flowers of the Caribbean
G. W. Lennox and S. A. Seddon, 1978, Macmillan Caribbean

Fruits and Vegetables of the Caribbean
M. J. Bourne, G. W. Lennox and S. A. Seddon, 1988, Macmillan Caribbean

Growing Orchids in the Caribbean
Marilyn Light, 1995, Macmillan Caribbean

Native Orchids of the Eastern Caribbean
Julian Kenny, 1988, Macmillan Caribbean

Trees of the Caribbean
S. A. Seddon and G. W. Lennox, 1980, Macmillan Caribbean

Wild Plants of Barbados
Sean Carrington, 1993, Macmillan Caribbean

Wild Plants of the Eastern Caribbean
Sean Carrington, 1997, Macmillan Caribbean

Index to plant names

Figures in *italics* refer to captions.

General index

Figures in *italics* refer to captions.